The Avocado Drive Zoo

Also by Earl Hamner

Spencer's Mountain
Fifty Roads to Town
You Can't Get There from Here
The Homecoming

The Avocado Drive Zoo

At Home with My Family and the Creatures We've Loved

Earl Hamner

CUMBERLAND HOUSE
NASHVILLE, TENNESSEE

Portions of this book were published in 1997 in *The Hollywood Zoo*.

Published by Cumberland House Publishing, Inc.
431 Harding Industrial Drive, Nashville, TN 37211.

Cover design: Gore Studios, Inc.
Illustrations on pages 13, 221 & 222: Jean Reese
Text design: Lisa Taylor

The Library of Congress has catalogued the hardcover edition as follows:
Library of Congress Cataloging-in-Publication Data

Hamner, Earl.
        The Avocado Drive zoo : at home with my family and the creatures
we've loved / by Earl Hamner.
            p.   cm.
        ISBN 1-58182-020-8 (hardcover : alk. paper)
        1. Hamner, Earl—Homes and haunts—California—Los Angeles.
2. Authors, American—20th century—Biography. 3. Television
producers and directors—United States—Biography. 4. Pet owners—
California—Los Angeles—Biography. 5. Wild animals as pets—
California—Los Angeles. 6. Authors's spouses—United States—
Biography. 7. Hamner, Jane.   I. Title
PS3558.A456Z464   1999
813'.54—dc21
        [b]   98-56398
                                                                  CIP

Printed in the United States of America
1 2 3 4 5 6 7 8 — 03 02 01 00 99 98

Dedicated to Sue Salter,
a charter member of the Zoo

Introduction

We fell in love with the house on Avocado Drive the first time we saw it. We were house hunting and had become lost in the Hollywood Hills. Eventually we happened to stumble across a pretty winding country road. When we saw the FOR SALE sign we parked the car and peered through the tall windows of the empty house. From the outside we could see high ceilings, a generous-sized living room, a fireplace, and a view that encompassed the entire San Fernando Valley.

Jane and I agreed on the spot that this was the house we had been searching for. We made a bid on it that very evening and within a few days we were in escrow. This is the house that became "home" with all the warmth and comfort the word implies.

During the coming years my career took off and my income doubled, then tripled, and finally reached a level that a Great Depression-raised youngster could never have imagined. We could have moved to a larger, more expensive house, to one with a larger swimming pool and a more prestigious address, but we were bonded with the house and the neighborhood.

It was here we raised our two children and lived with an enormous number of household pets as well as wildlife that occasionally became part of our lives.

These stories were written during the happiest days of my life. I hope you enjoy reading them as much as I have enjoyed living them and writing about them.

The Avocado Drive Zoo

1. Hero Adored by Beautiful Women!
Falls in Love!

When I was a boy growing up in the Blue Ridge Mountains of Virginia during the Great Depression I was filled with dreams. My dreams were fired by the books I read, and while my body was chopping wood or milking the family cow, my mind was strolling down the Champs-Élysées, swimming at Malibu, signing autographs at Sardi's, having tea at the London Ritz, or hailing my gondola in front of The Royal Danelli. Most of all in my fantasy life, I dreamed of becoming a writer.

All of these dreams have come true, and they began to materialize in 1953. It was a year of many landmarks in my life.

Random House had just published my first novel, *Fifty Roads to Town*. The reviews were good, and a few copies had been sold. I suspect they were bought primarily by friends, but still I felt good. I had known the exhilaration of holding the book in my hands. I had finally arrived as a real writer. I was a success!

Success brought remarkably little money. But there were other rewards such as a good review in the *New York Times*! It also brought its share of disappointment such as going in Scribners and asking for the book only to find that they had never heard of it. It was at that point that I decided it would be wise to hold on to my job as a scriptwriter at the National Broadcasting Company.

All around me my friends were getting married and having children. They would invite me over to see the baby and at nine-thirty the father, who would once have been a drinking companion until the last bar closed for the night, would now begin to yawn and make noises about having to take the four o'clock feeding! What happened to the women was even worse. Beautiful young things who used to dance until the Rainbow Room closed and then take the ferry to Staten Island to watch the sun come up, these lovely sinful young women overnight became saintly and maternal, seemingly interested only in the merits of formula over breast feeding.

I resolved never to get married. Life was too full to be burdened with children, responsibility, and routine. I would write more books. I would travel. Perhaps I would live in Europe. I had lived in Paris for a while after World War II and I imagined myself returning there to a cozy little apartment where I would write my novels under a skylight and go to sleep at night to the music of an accordion playing a song about the joys of being young and drinking the white wine in Nogent.

And then one evening I left my office at NBC where I had been preparing an interview to be featured the next morning on *The Today Show*. I was on my way to a restaurant on Forty-seventh Street to have a drink with my friends Noah and Sherry. On my way to join them I stopped at a table to say hello to Susanne Salter, a friend from the publicity department at NBC.

"I'd like you to meet my roommate, Jane Martin," said Susie.

As my Italian cousins are wont to say, "The earth moved." Only later when I was more coherent was I able to remember details. She was blonde. She wore her hair in a bun. Her eyes were blue and when she smiled the whole room was illuminated. I could go on but she will read these words and will be embarrassed. To be conservative, in my estimation she was the most beautiful woman I had ever seen.

I later had the impression that I made several brilliant remarks befitting a young novelist. But Jane and Susie to this day insist that I spoke not a word.

What I *am* sure of is that when I reached Sherry and Noah's table, I said, "I have just met the girl I am going to marry."

The psychologists claim there is no such thing as love at first sight. They claim that when two people "fall in love" what really happens is that the two lovers recognize a myriad of interlocking needs—psychological, sexual, social, economic, spiritual, etc. I'm not sure I go along with all of that, but I do know that one of the qualities that I recognized in Jane was an overwhelming compassion for all of life and that she recognized in me a positive response to her feelings.

Jane had recently lost a cocker spaniel named Stormy. He had been devoted to Jane. He was fiercely protective of her and if anyone came near her he would bite.

"The janitor has been very nice about it," she said. "But the delivery man from Gristede's has sued."

"Did you ever think of getting him a muzzle?" I asked.

"I got him one," she answered, "but he wouldn't wear it."

"Didn't you ever try to make him wear it?" I asked.

"Oh," she said, "nobody could ever make Stormy do anything he didn't want to do."

Stormy had bitten a good number of people, and Jane had spent a lot of time at the Bite Division on the Upper East Side. That was where Stormy had to be registered as a "biter" and be examined for rabies every time he bit another person.

Now he was dead and Jane grieved for him. She swore she would never have another dog. And then one day she was walking along Sixth Avenue and just happened to glance in the window of the pet shop.

And she saw Clemmentine.

Clemmentine was seven weeks old. She had long, brownish-blonde hair and soulful eyes. She had already perfected the old cocker spaniel trick of gazing out of the window with such longing that even people who knew better were tempted to take her home.

After she spotted the puppy in the window, Jane began

walking home on the other side of the street so she would
not have to meet those wistful eyes. It was not long before
she was walking along the west side of Sixth Avenue again
and allowing herself just one glance at the puppy before continuing on to the apartment on Twelfth Street.

There came a day when she could resist no longer. She
stopped and knelt down so that she was eye level with the
pup. Knowing damn well what it was doing, the puppy
pressed its nose to the window. Whatever mysterious bond
that is formed between a dog and his special person was
cemented at that moment. It was further strengthened
when Jane entered the shop and asked permission to hold
the puppy.

At dinner that evening Jane confessed to Susie that she
had lost control of herself, that she had held the dog and
could not live without her.

"Why don't you buy her?" asked Susie.

"Thirty dollars," answered Jane. "I don't have it."

"Neither do I. Not if we're going to make the rent next
month."

"Maybe I'll drink a martini," said Jane.

"I don't think getting drunk is the answer," said Susie.

"Oh, I don't mean to get drunk," said Jane. "But a martini
might give me the courage to call home and ask for the thirty
dollars."

The drunken appeal to Davenport, Iowa, was averted
when Susie called me.

"Janie-Poo's gone lunatic over that puppy in the pet

shop on Sixth Avenue. I think she'll absolutely perish if she doesn't get it."

Susie invents and uses language imaginatively. Jane often became "Janie-Poo." I am a staid-looking, buttoned-down person, the last man alive one would call "The Pearl," but Susie sees no inconsistency in calling me "Earl the Pearl."

"Why doesn't she buy it?" I asked.

Susie explained about the thirty dollars and the rent.

"Why don't we each pitch in ten bucks and surprise her with it?"

"That's only twenty," said Sue.

"We could hit J. Dale for the other ten. He's rolling in money."

J. Dale was an associate producer on *The Tonight Show* and sure enough, when Susie hit him up for the ten, he agreed to pitch in.

The three of us picked up the puppy. On our way to the apartment she peed on me twice. It was a pattern that would continue till the end of her days, for she was a nervous and erratic dog and the only way she seemed able to cope with life's crises was to relieve herself wherever she might be.

Susie had made sure that Jane would still be at the apartment. We arrived, opened the door, put the puppy inside and stood waiting out in the hall.

For a long moment nothing happened. And then we heard a surprised shriek followed by low crooning noises, and finally the suggestion of a sob. Knowing the grief Jane had suffered over the death of Stormy, we withdrew.

"How about a drink?" suggested Susie.

"Ice Bar's just around the corner," said J. Dale.

"Let's go," I said.

The Ice Bar was not really the name of the saloon. Jane and Susie called it that because they had made friends with the Irish bartender, and he would provide them with free ice when there was a party or when their refrigerator broke down.

"I'll have a Sazerac," said Sue to the bartender when we found a place at the bar. She was forever learning about fancy drinks uptown and then ordering them in the local bars where an order for anything more complicated than a bourbon and water would raise a blank stare from the bartender.

But this bartender had already been won over, and following Susie's directions, he began mixing her Sazerac. Finally, when we each had been served and taken a sip of our drinks, Susie turned to J. Dale and me and said: "What are we going to do about Janie-Poo?"

"Why do we have to do anything about her?"

"Well," said Sue, "she went home for Christmas."

You learned after a while to hear Susie out. A simple declarative sentence might announce a theme, and then variations would gradually emerge until finally the full body of her meaning would become clear. J. Dale and I listened patiently.

"She had that terrific job as an editor at *Harper's Bazaar*, but they wouldn't give her any time off for Christmas. So she took it anyway, and they fired her. And then she found something with the Yellow Cab Company, but the drivers all got in fights over which one got to give her a ride home, and now she's doing research and has to sit in that gloomy old public library writing down things when everybody else is out having a divine time. What are we going to do about her?"

"If she'll have me, I would like to marry her," I said.

"Oh, Pearl!" screamed Susie. "What a perfect solution!"

"Oh, I'm not doing it to solve anything," I said. "It's just that I'm in love with her."

Following that, Susie cried and J. Dale ordered another round of Sazeracs. We were all busy toasting one another when Jane slipped in and joined us at the bar. She carried the cocker spaniel puppy, which had already lost its look of longing and taken on a secure, if not downright smug expression.

"Her name is Clemmentine," said Jane, "like in the song 'Oh, My Darling.'"

"Janie-Poo," exclaimed Susie, "Pearl wants to marry you."

"Well, all right," said Jane, and when I leaned over to kiss her, Clemmentine bit me. She was already a one-person dog, and I wasn't the person.

2. *Hero Enters Matrimony!*

Jane and I were married the following October. Jane was a lapsed Catholic and I was a renegade Episcopalian, but we somehow arranged to have the union blessed at St. Bartholomew's on Park Avenue. Before the reception we were concerned about how the hill clan from Virginia and the Scotch-Irish Davenport, Iowans would react. We need not have worried. They were tentative at first, but as the champagne worked its magic, they became "kissing cousins." I have never found out for sure, but there is suspicion that my father and Jane's aunt Minnie became even better acquainted. All I can remember is that as Jane and I were leaving the reception, I could see my father's hand resting affectionately on Aunt Minnie's knee.

Our first apartment was in a professional building on West Thirteenth Street. It consisted of two large rooms connected by a stairway. The "living room" had a window that reached from the floor to the ceiling and afforded a magnificent view of downtown Manhattan. The view made up somewhat for the fact that there was no kitchen and that the bathroom was a converted darkroom, for the apartment had been occupied by a photographer who had used it as his studio. The upstairs room had a skylight over the entire ceiling. The ceiling leaked when it rained and since the only piece of furniture we owned was the bed, we simply moved it around the room until we found a dry spot.

We thought we were as close to heaven as two people could be. Soon after we moved in, Aunt Eloise, a pretentious relative by marriage, came to town. We were so proud of our new home that we invited her to stop by for a drink. After riding the cantankerous elevator up to our lofty digs, she exclaimed, "Oh, you live in the attic!" And she carried this information back to Jane's family in Iowa.

After word reached Iowa that Jane was "living in poverty," her ever-supportive family responded generously. Checks arrived, and we began to accumulate possessions. Jane was a genius at invention. One end of the bathroom became a kitchen, and since there wasn't room for a real stove, she made a stacking arrangement of a toaster oven, a portable baking oven, and a hot plate, all resting on top of a miniature clothes washer and dryer.

Clemmentine grew increasingly antisocial. She became moody and would sit and stare thoughtfully at things only she could see for long periods of time. Occasionally she would go into a trance and communicate with the beyond. She growled in her sleep. She developed a fondness for garbage. On our weekend outings at Fire Island when the other citizens were proudly walking their haughty Afghans or their elegantly clipped poodles, we would be dragging Clemmentine away from some rotten fish she had found. She would bite anyone she could get to, especially if she felt that person was threatening to Jane.

Clemmentine was never happy in the apartment. To take her on her walks, we had to drag her onto the elevator. Its creaks and groans would alarm her so that she would cringe at our feet, pee, and whine piteously until we picked her up. We were sure it was her anxieties that led her to have a voracious appetite, so we fed her more than we should. Her appetite increased. She became grossly fat.

My fame as a novelist faded quickly and while the novel sold its first printing, there was not enough interest to keep the book in print. Fortunately I had kept my job as a staff writer at the National Broadcasting Company.

At night, during lunch hours, and sometimes early in the morning, I took the advice of Belle Becker, my editor at Random House, and started a new novel.

I wasn't quite sure what the new novel was about. I knew vaguely that it was inspired by the security my father gave his family with his dream of building a house for us. His dream, plus my own dream of attending college, and the ironic way I eventually got there, became the plot of what evolved into a book called *Spencer's Mountain*. I had no idea when I was writing it that the book would change my life.

"We're having a party!" Jane announced one evening when I arrived home.

"Big one?" I asked.

"Very small. Very intimate," she announced. "It's just going to be you and me and Susie and Dale."

She had bought flowers, set out some rather grand champagne glasses we had received as wedding gifts, and had champagne cooling in the silver ice bucket. The candle-light concealed the fact that our new sofa, a marble coffee table, and some cushions were the only furnishings in the room. Still the view of the downtown Manhattan skyline was breathtaking, and in her long hostess skirt Jane was most elegant.

"You are one gorgeous tomato," I told her.

"Last night you called me a gorgeous broad."

"Last night I was horny."

"Go get dressed," she ordered. "Something nice."

"How formal is this dinner?" I asked.

"I did sort of tell Sue and Dale to dress up," she said. "Since it's our first party, it ought to be something to remember."

Proudly Jane showed off what she was going to serve for dinner. It was all cooked, all laid out on an ironing board she had converted into a serving table. The main dish was a small turkey she had roasted in the portable oven. There was corn bread stuffing, thick white French asparagus she had found at Balducci's, a corn soufflé, baby haricots vert, and yeasty dinner rolls all ready to pop in the toaster oven. In honor of my Southern background, she had made a sweet-potato pie for dessert.

I went upstairs to change into something more formal and by the time I got back down to the living room Susie and Dale had arrived. Susie had on an elegant black outfit and pearls. Dale wore his tuxedo.

"Oh, Pearl, you look divine," shrieked Susie when I came into the room.

"I am divine," I answered. "When are you going to become a Mormon so I can marry you, too?"

"Why would I want to be a Mormon?"

"So I can marry you, too."

"Oh, we're already married, Pearl," said Susie. "That day at St. Bartholomew's I said the vows right along with Janie. I'm yours."

"I don't think I like that very much," said Jane.

"I don't see why not," said Susie wickedly. "Didn't I practically propose to him for us?"

"Oh, he would have gotten around to it in time," said Jane.

"You're just lucky I proposed for you. I could have asked him to marry me!"

"Ignore her," said Dale, who had poured the champagne. "She's just trying to make me jealous."

We drifted to the tall window and watched night fall across lower Manhattan. We reminisced about our early days in New York. Jane and Susie told about their first night in town when they found they had rented a roach-infested apartment and moved immediately to the Plaza until something better could be located. Dale told about his first week in town when he had found work dressing as an Easter rabbit and posing for photographs with children at Macy's. I reminisced about being down to my last two dollars on Christmas Eve, spending it on a loaf of bread and a tin of sardines, only to have the key to the sardine can break off, forcing me to tear it open with a pair of scissors. We finished the bottle of champagne.

Jane announced, "I think dinner is ready."

Dinner was indeed ready, but not for us. When we turned to the impromptu serving board, we saw Clemmentine. She had somehow gotten up on the ironing board. Most of the turkey was gone and a lot of the stuffing. Only the asparagus and haricots vert remained untouched. Most of the sweet potato pie was smeared on Clemmentine's face.

I looked to Jane. For a moment I worried that she might burst into tears now that her first dinner party had been ruined.

"It's all right, honey!" I said in an attempt at consolation.

Clemmentine belched.

Jane began to laugh. Susie began to laugh. Dale began to laugh and they were all still laughing when we reached the Ice Bar and ordered hamburgers. Susie ordered a Sazerac. Dale ordered beer, I ordered a boilermaker, and Jane ordered milk.

"I thought you hated milk!"

"I do," she said. "But I have to think of the baby."

"Oh mi-God," hollered Susie. "We're pregnant!"

"I think they just heard you in Michigan," said Dale.

"I don't care if they heard me in Montana," said Susie. "I've wanted to have a baby since I was thirteen. Have you seen the doctor yet?"

"Just this morning. The baby's due in May!"

Jane sailed right through the pregnancy, but Susie had morning sickness for the first two months.

I became reverent of Jane. She seemed touched by God, a holy vessel courageously carrying my child, our hope for the future of the world, my sweetheart turned Earth Mother. One night I woke and found her sitting in the bay window. The moonlight softly illuminated her face, and in her white gown and with her blonde hair she looked so holy, so rapt in her reverie that I hardly dared intrude. When I finally did, I asked, "Are you thinking noble thoughts?"

"Actually, I was wondering why I have to pee all the time," she answered.

We worried about Clemmentine. She was already so neurotic that we felt that a baby might just send her totally round the bend.

"Maybe a puppy," Jane suggested. "A companion, something so she won't be jealous of the baby."

We had to go all the way to Staten Island for Chloe. She was a black cocker spaniel, mostly ears and feet. Clem had no idea what to make of her.

Clem at first pretended Chloe wasn't there at all. She would gaze beyond her, over her head, through her. It was as if Clem were saying to us, "You wouldn't really do this to me!"

Chloe would try to get Clem to play with her, but that didn't work either. In time, Clem retreated under the bed and would come out only at mealtime or for her walk. Once she finished her food or we returned from her walk, she would scram under the bed and remain there. If we looked in on her, she growled.

"I think she's hiding something under there," said Jane.

What she was hiding, it turned out, was an old sock, which she was mothering, for when we finally took her to the vet, he announced that Clem had developed a false pregnancy.

And while Susie suffered morning sickness and Clemmentine nursed old socks, Jane sailed through with a minimum of dramatics.

Jane's mother came to be with us when the birth date drew near. One day she called me to say that she and Jane were already at Doctor's Hospital, and I hurried there. The baby arrived before I did.

"You have a son," said Dr. Sivigney, and in a life that had known a great many elated moments, nothing could quite reach the thrill and pride and ineffable joy I felt.

Jane's mother and I found the viewing window, and there was Scott, a perfect little being, blissfully asleep. It was a solemn moment, and I thought that of all of life's gifts, none could be greater than this.

"Has he got everything he's supposed to have?" asked Jane.

"Double," I answered. "Two of everything. Thank you for him! You are not just a gorgeous tomato, you are a holy vessel! Bless you!"

"Stay with Earl tonight, Mother," pleaded Jane. "I've seen him like this, and anything can happen."

"Nothing's going to happen," I assured her. "We're just going to stop by the Meditation Chapel at the United Nations."

"For God's sake, why?" asked Jane.

"We're going to give thanks for this miracle," I answered. "What place could be more appropriate than the United Nations?"

"You see what I mean, Mother?" said Jane.

"I'll look after him," her mother promised.

After thanking God for my son at the United Nations, we proceeded to St. Patrick's Cathedral and while Jane's mother waited patiently at the back, I gave thanks at the altar. I was lurching toward a cab when Jane's mother took me by the arm and brought me to a halt.

"What are you up to now?" she demanded.

"We should stop for a minute at St. Bartholomew's," I said. "It's where we were married."

"I was there," she said.

"It's only a few blocks away," I said.

"I'm not going another step without a drink," she declared.

We were not far from Forty-ninth Street and Sixth Avenue. We were close to a very special place to me. We were very near to Hurley's.

"Can we get a drink there?" she asked.

I assured her we could.

"Then what are we waiting for?"

And off we went.

It would be wrong to call Hurley's a bar. It was more like a club, a home away from home, a convenient place to meet friends, a haven where those of us who were regulars felt an intense sense of belonging. It was a refuge, not unlike Cheers, the watering place on the television show, a little less grand perhaps, with a little touch of show business early in the evening, a little more Irish as the night progressed.

Connie Hurley, the owner, was a dour man. He would cash a check, scramble an egg, and routinely serve up whatever was ordered, editorializing a bit with a lifted eyebrow if someone ordered something as esoteric as a "pink lady" or a "creme de menthe frappé." He would make and serve such things, but the look that went with the service was hardly worth it.

Connie's smile had been dulled by the burdens and perplexities of life on the corner of Forty-ninth Street and Sixth Avenue, but he smiled that night when I told him that I had become a father.

Two years later, I was called to Doctor's Hospital again. Jane had already gone into the labor room and her mother and I sat together. By this time, my mother-in-law had begun to regard me with a certain amount of mistrust if she felt I was under stress.

It was not long before Dr. Sivigney came out and announced, "You have a daughter!"

I did not think that life could hold such joy for me twice, but when I saw Caroline, I reached such dizzying heights of elation that even the doctor looked as if he might have to administer first aid.

"Is he all right?" he asked my mother-in-law.

"We're never sure," said Jane's mother.

After we said goodnight to Jane, we headed for the exit. Her mother laid her hand on my arm.

"I just want you to know," she said, "that you are not going to drag me all over New York City going from one cathedral to another all night long."

This time we went straight to Hurley's.

"Her name is Caroline," I told Connie Hurley. And for the second time since I met him, Connie smiled.

3. Transplanted Turtles Turn Town Topsy-Turvy! Tabloids Tattle!

In the summer of 1960, Scott and I visited my family in Schuyler, Virginia. Schuyler was once described in a guide book as "a hamlet in the Blue Ridge that rises to mild hilarity on Saturday night." It is about twenty-eight miles south of Charlottesville in an area called "The Ragged Mountains," just where the hills begin to climb upward toward the Blue Ridge Mountains. Today it is shown on maps of Virginia as the location of The Walton Museum, and is visited by tourists from all over the world.

I think it is generally known that my family was the model for the family known to television viewers as the Waltons. Even today, after the series has been off network television for some years, my mother and father's house, the church, and the general store are tourist attractions, visited by thousands of people yearly.

Our family home is not very different from the one represented on the television series—a modest, white clapboard farmhouse with a porch stretching across the front. Oaks and maples grace the long front lawn and a cement walkway curves from the front steps to a wisteria arch at the front gate. Chipmunks nest in cracks in the cement near the curve in the walkway. In the early spring, my mother's beds of yellow, white, and blue crocuses are landmarks. The bulbs have multiplied over the years so that the blossoms are thick and rich. They make a spectacular show of color, often reaching up through the snow to display themselves.

That summer when Scott and I visited Schuyler, my mother and father were still alive. They were remarkable people and I don't think they ever got used to being models for characters I wrote about in my novels and television scripts.

In time, my mother was to be portrayed by Maureen O'Hara in *Spencer's Mountain*, by Patricia Neal in *The Homecoming*, by Teresa Wright in *Appalachian Autumn*, and by Michael Learned in *The Waltons*.

My father did live to see himself portrayed by Henry Fonda and Andy Duggan, but he did not live long enough to see Ralph Waite's memorable portrayal of him on *The Waltons*.

My father was a hunter, a fisherman, and a dramatist. While Scott and I were there, on one of our rambles through the woods my father managed to transform an abandoned log cabin we chanced upon into the place where in earlier years you could buy the best moonshine in the mountains. Under the old cabin, my father claimed, lived a nest of rattlesnakes, "some as big around as your leg." A hip-high rock with a curious bowl-like indentation in it, he swore to be Pocahontas's Throne. A quiet pond where no fish had lived for a hundred years was promised to be the place where the "granddaddy of all catfish lived." I knew he was boasting and showing off to endear himself to my son, and I loved him for that, but I suspected there wasn't a shred of truth in what he said.

Well, maybe. As it turned out there might have been just a little truth to the snake story. And there could have been some justification for the suggestion that the cabin had been occupied by a bootlegger.

Some years after my father died in 1969, I retraced that walk we had taken. There were still no fish in that quiet pond. At least none accepted the bait I offered them. And Pocahontas's Throne had disappeared. Maybe it really had been an Indian artifact and quite possibly rests today in some museum or private collection of Indian art. But I did take special note that underneath the old log cabin that my father claimed to have been the haunt of moonshiners, I spotted, in good condition, an antique spool bedstead. I started to crawl under the cabin to retrieve it, but my way was blocked by a fair-sized rattlesnake. The rattlesnake hastened my departure, but before I withdrew entirely from the crawlspace, I spotted several shelves, each of them filled with a clear white liquid.

Recently I visited the site again. The old log cabin had fallen in upon itself, and was covered with lichen and ferns. The woodland was reclaiming the logs that it had given to the original owner. Somewhere under that pile of rotting logs may rest a few Mason jars of the best moonshine my father ever tasted. And perhaps a rattlesnake or two. I'll never know for sure.

When our visit to Schuyler was over, Scott and I headed for Richmond to visit with my brothers and sisters and Scott's first and second and third cousins. We took Route 6 the old River Road, which skirts the James River. In Colonial times, it had been the pathway for the shipment of farm and forest products from Buckingham, Nelson, and Albemarle Counties down to the capitol at Williamsburg.

Shortly, the first of the turtles began to appear. They were Eastern box turtles. They ranged in diameter from the size of a quarter to eight or ten inches. They were predominantly yellow, orange, and brown in color with solemn, beaknosed faces, five-toed feet, and scaly skin. They are shy creatures and their facial expression is very much like that of Steven Spielberg's "E.T."

When we spotted the first one, Scott admonished me to be careful and not to run over it. It was not a warning I needed. We are extraordinarily tuned in to animals in our family. Crushing the fragile and well-designed carapace of box turtle by running over them is not my idea of sport. Others, however, found it "fun."

Some motorists, rather than maneuvering around th

urtles, elected to run over them, leaving behind the crushed emains of an ancient, complicated, and extraordinary xample of one way life chooses to express itself.

Eventually we saw a motorist deliberately go out of his vay to murder a turtle. The pickup truck that was traveling head of us at one point swerved over to the opposite lane, nd when we arrived at that point we could see why. He had een aiming for a turtle. The shell had been flattened and the ontents smashed into a quivering blob.

"Why did he do that?" asked Scott indignantly.

"Some people are just that way," I answered. "They like o kill things."

"I don't understand that," said Scott.

"Neither do I," I replied.

"If we could get ahead of that truck and get to the turtles efore he does, we could save them," said Scott.

We had gone several miles before we spotted another urtle. It had ventured about three feet onto the highway on ne right-hand side. It held its head high and was progress-ng in its slow lurch toward the center of the road. I put my oot on the brake and came to a stop only two or three feet way from the turtle.

"They don't bite, do they?" asked Scott as he was getting ut of the car.

"He'll just clamp his shell together," I said. "Go get him."

Scott touched the turtle tentatively and when he did, it vithdrew its head and feet and clamped its carapace and lastron together.

"Got him," said Scott as he jumped back in the car.

By the time we reached Richmond, we had a collection of twelve box turtles of assorted sizes. Since we had nothing to contain them, they were corralled on the floor in the front of the car where they remained motionless, their shells tightly clamped together.

"How was Virginia?" asked Jane when we arrived home to our new apartment. We had been lucky enough to find a garden apartment at 44 West Twelfth Street. The apartment boasted two unusual features for apartments of that modest price range. One was a garden, and the other was what had been at one time a back porch. Some former tenant had completely enclosed the porch in glass. To make room for Scott and Caroline, Jane and I had made the glass room our bedroom, and what had been our bedroom became the nursery.

"We brought some Virginians home with us," I announced. We opened the shopping bag and showed her the twelve turtles.

"What are we going to do with them?" demanded Jane darkly.

"We're going to release them in the garden," I said grandly. "Give the place some character."

"I like this one," said Caroline, picking up the one the size of a quarter. "I'm going to name her Susie Green." Susie Green was Caroline's favorite sitter. She named several of her childhood pets after Susie Green.

"It's not a *she*," said Scott. "It's a he."

"How do you know, smartie?" demanded Caroline.

"He looks like a he," answered Scott.

"Well, I'm going to name him Susie Green anyway," rejoined Caroline.

"They are kind of cute," said Jane, softening as she held the smallest one. It was hardly larger than a quarter and when it opened its shell long enough to gaze up at her with its shy, inquisitive eyes, Jane was completely won over.

"Let's let them loose," suggested Caroline, and in short order, Scott and Caroline and their friends, Madeline and Clemmo Robbins from the adjoining garden, were enraptured as the immigrant turtles wandered off to whatever part of the garden that pleased them.

"What do they eat?" asked Jane.

"Oh, they'll forage for themselves," I said. "They're accustomed to finding their own food in the wild."

"But they're not in the wild now," said Jane sensibly. "They're in the middle of New York City."

"Oh, I'll plant a wild area for them," I promised. "Pine trees and trilliums, plantain and dandelions, things like that."

"Good," said Jane knowingly. "In the meantime, I'll find them some lettuce."

"Oh, I'll plant that, too," I said.

"Until it comes up, I'll just get some from the refrigerator."

The turtles liked the lettuce and through experimentation we found they also enjoyed hamburger, tomatoes, bits of steak, carrot tops, spinach, and almost any leafy green vegetable.

We named them "The Virginia Colony," after the first

permanent settlement at Jamestown, and they seemed perfectly happy as they made themselves at home at 44 West Twelfth Street. There was no way they could know or care that soon they were destined to attain the dream of many East Coast residents—they were going to become Californians. They were soon to become charter members of what became known as "The Avocado Drive Zoo."

4. Awful Event at JFK.
Why He Had to Leave New York!

It was Christmas of 1960, and our lives would never again be the same.

The holiday was tinged with sadness for we knew it would be the last one we would spend as residents of New York. We would no longer be a part of that incredible city. We would no longer be "New Yorkers."

In a few days we would be saying good-bye to what a friend of mine always referred to as "the big time." In those post–World War II days I think what he meant was simply that New York was the place where the best of us came to sing or to write or to dance or to act, to give of whatever talent we might have. If it was a talent that made us different, it also made us a little too big for the hometown we had left. We brought our talents there like gifts and laid them at the foot of the city. I had done that as a writer and Jane had done that as an editor and decorator. And now, as difficult as the idea was for us to accept, the city would simply have to try to get along without us.

We had come there as carefree, adventuresome young people. We were leaving with "responsibilities" in the form of one son, one daughter, two dogs, and a family of turtles. We were only taking one of the turtles to California right away, the wakeful one Scott had named Hoaker. He had refused to hibernate, and when the weather turned severe we brought him indoors and kept him in a box under the refrigerator. The other eleven were hibernating somewhere in the garden at 44 West Twelfth Street. We decided that we would retrieve them on some future trip back to New York when the ground was thawed and the turtles were more accessible than they were at the moment. We had already written a note to the next occupants, and left it on the mantel. It was to alert them so they would not be too shocked when spring came and they discovered a colony of recently thawed-out and ravenously hungry turtles in their backyard.

On New Year's Day we watched the Rose Parade broadcast from Pasadena. The sunshine seemed to spill right out of the television set and into that small, dark ground-floor apartment. It seemed to assure us that our future was comfortable and that fame and richness were within our grasp, waiting there for the taking in California.

The first lap of our journey to California was to be to Davenport, Iowa. There Jane, Scott, Caroline, the dogs, and Hoaker were to wait with Jane's family, while I went on to Los Angeles to rent a house, buy a car, and find work.

The first week of January we shipped all of our furniture to Los Angeles, had a grand party in the empty apartment, and the next day with the two children, the two dogs, and our luggage, which included a Dobbs hat box containing Hoaker, the wakeful turtle, we set out for the airport.

In spite of the sunshine we had seen on television, I was apprehensive about the trip. I had a family dependent on me. I had burned my bridges behind me in New York. I knew practically nobody in Hollywood, and very little about film. Equally alarming was the fact that the amount of money with which I was to rent a house, buy a car, and live on until I found a job was quickly shrinking. The cost of shipping our furniture to the West Coast alone was incredible. At least it seemed so to one country boy whose father had paid only five hundred dollars during the depression for an entire house.

I had one hope for the future. The literary agent Don Congdon had agreed to represent my work, and he would be showing the manuscript of my new novel to the New York publishers.

Don had read the manuscript of *Spencer's Mountain* and I suspected that, in addition to the merits of the book, he felt a kinship to the material because of some similarities in our backgrounds. We were both products of the Depression, came from people of modest backgrounds, and from areas of the country where young men, more often than not, followed their fathers into mines or quarries to make a living. *Spencer's Mountain* was the story of one young man's struggle to break that pattern, to become the first in his family to attend college, to break out of a restrictive society and to make something of himself.

Congdon represented such fabled writers as Ray Bradbury, William Manchester, Lillian Hellman, Edward Abby, and William Stryon. I was honored and encouraged to be in such company. And having someone like Don enthusiastically looking after my literary affairs gave me the courage to make the dramatic change I had now undertaken in my life.

I tend to misplace things like airplane tickets, so we had learned that it is best for Jane to be in charge of travel details. At the airline counter Jane presented our tickets to the efficient young man there whose name plate read Donald-R. Donald-R was short and blond, but the volume and timbre of his voice were so magnificent that anyone hearing it was intimidated and awed.

When Donald-R noticed that we had requested a container in which we were to transport Clemmentine and Chloe, the two cocker spaniels, he announced that he personally would see us through the difficulties. He went so far in assuring us of his commitment to us that I began to worry that he might accompany us all the way to California. We stood aside for the other passengers while Donald-R went to locate the crates for the dogs. Scott and Caroline at that moment were waiting patiently where we had placed them in the waiting area. All seemed well. The airline people were smiling and patient with the brave pioneer family that was making the trek to the West Coast.

Donald-R came back with the crates for the dogs, but neither Clem nor Chloe would enter them. We pushed and coaxed, but they dug in their feet in such a way that there was simply no forcing them. At such a time Chloe had an especially malevolent look that she reserved for me, and she gave it to me now.

Thinking that Jane had turned away and could not see me, I gave Chloe a poke with my toe.

"I saw you kick that dog!" said Jane.

"It was a poke, not a kick," I insisted. "And I may murder the both of them if they don't get in their cages!"

"It's not going to do any of us any good for you to lose your temper," said Jane. "Why don't you just go for a walk? Donald-R and I will get them settled in."

I hope they bite Donald-R in the patootie, I thought, but still he seemed to know his way around situations of this kind and I was perfectly content to leave this one in his hands. I strolled off to the window to watch the planes taking off. On the way I passed Scott and Caroline who were playing with Hoaker, the wakeful turtle. They had taken him out of the Dobbs hat box and were allowing him to plod from one of them to the other. I smiled at them and thought what grand children we had produced. How happy we were all going to be in California! What a fine wife Jane was to protect me from my volcanic temper. What a marvelous adventure we were having!

Satisfied that I had my temper under control I walked back to the counter. Clemmentine and Chloe now cringed in their crates. Clemmentine, as she always did when she was nervous, had already defecated. Chloe was baring her teeth at the world in general, but the important thing had been accomplished. They were both in their crates and ready for shipment to Iowa.

It was one of those moments that we experience when we are young. There comes a sudden surge of exuberance, a joy so intense that we do unreasonable and romantic things. There was little justification for it, except for the fact that I was engulfed with love and joy. In the middle of the airport terminal I threw my arms around Jane and announced solemnly:

"Do you realize that this is a moment that will never come again?"

"Good," said Jane. "I don't think I could live through it twice."

"No," I objected. "Don't joke. It's a milestone, a land mark in our lives. From this day on, we will measure time before and after the day we left New York for California."

"The reptile is not going to California," said the Donald-R regretfully. "It's going to have to stay here."

"What reptile are you talking about?" I asked, trying to give a dangerous edge to my voice.

"That reptile your children were playing with," said Donald-R.

"That is not a reptile," I said in the grand manner. "That is a Virginia box turtle!"

"It is a reptile, and FAA regulations forbid reptiles to travel in the passenger compartment." Donald-R folded his arms and observed me defiantly. "It is definitely not going to fly out of here."

"Like hell it is not!" I shouted. "That turtle is a member of the family and it goes where we go!"

"Earl!" said Jane in what I had learned to recognize as her tactful voice. "You're beginning to attract a crowd."

"Good," I shouted. "We will need witnesses for the lawsuit!" I looked around, hoping to find a number of supportive faces. What I saw instead was a long line of passengers eyeing me belligerently.

It was then that Jane asked if I had seen the children.

"They were over by Gate 8 a second ago," I said.

"The plane at Gate 8 just left for Omaha," said Donald-R.

"They were probably on it," I shouted and went running down the corridor in search of my children. I found them at the next bay where they were happily dismantling a mock-up of an airplane that was part of a window display.

"Come away," I said without looking at them, hoping that the strolling policeman who was patrolling the area would not associate them with me.

"We're trying to decide what makes the propeller work," said Scott.

"It's probably a rubber band," I said. "Now come, we are going to Iowa."

"It's definitely not a rubber band," observed Caroline, removing a small box of computer parts from the display. "It looks more like a computer chip."

"What are you doing with those computer guts?" I shouted.

"You always told us to investigate before forming an

opinion," rejoined Caroline. "I was just doing what I was told. I didn't know the whole darn thing would fall apart."

Dragging the children, one by each hand, I returned to the counter where an enormous line of people looked at me with ill-concealed hatred. Even our friendly Donald-R seemed to have lost his sense of humor. Perhaps it had to do with the fact that Clem and Chloe had both lost control of their bladders and a stream of urine now flowed from their crates.

"Francine!" shouted Donald-R.

In response to his desperate cry, a uniformed, roaming ticket agent appeared.

"Yes, Donald?" she said.

"These are the Hamners," he said. "Would you see them on board, help them fasten themselves into their seats, and remain at the gate until the plane takes off and they are safely on their way."

"What about the reptile?" she asked as she watched Scott returning Hoaker to his hat box.

"It's a member of the family!" said Donald-R. "Where they go, it goes!"

I tried to shake his hand and thank Donald-R for his kindness, but his indignant glare suggested that he would prefer that we simply board the plane.

We were on our way to Hollywood at last, but first there was Iowa!

5. Disturbing Events in Iowa Questioned Sharply by Wife's Relatives! Why Hero Had to Leave Iowa!

It was good to be back in Iowa!

Most of the people in my business are contemptuous of Iowa, as they are of the Midwest in general. The closest most of my show-business friends have ever been to the place is to fly over it when they "sky" back and forth between New York and Los Angeles. They refer to it as the place where "Will they get it in . . . ?"

If my colleagues in the industry would look down from their planes, they would see what the WPA Guide to Iowa describes as ". . . level land, a region of subtly varying contours, where yellow light spreads over the great expanses and plays through the luxurious vegetation. Fields of corn and other grains are planted in even squares and rectangles. Groves of trees shelter the farm buildings. Large herds of stock feed in the knolly pasture lands. Sudden breaks in this level country are the low river valleys, from one to ten miles wide and covered by natural woodlands that rise in irregular lines of hills and bluffs at the valley's edge."

Jane's family home was a fine old Victorian mansion majestically situated on a bluff overlooking the Mississippi River. Jane's grandfather and his brothers had emigrated from Wanlochead, Scotland, in the early 1800s. They found work in Illinois as coal miners. With their Scottish devotion to industry and thrift, they ended up owning not only the coal mine but the little town around it, which they promptly renamed after themselves. As a reward for a lifetime of hard work, the grandfather, or "Faither" as he is still called, moved his family to Davenport, Iowa, where he bought a stately home that had been built in 1871 by Ambrose Copperwaithe Fulton.

I had first visited Davenport when Jane took me there to be looked over by her family. You don't find houses like 1206 East River Drive anymore. Regretfully it has gone out of the family now. It has become a bed and breakfast called "Fulton's Landing," and is listed on the National Register of Historic Places. It still has a great deal of charm, and the same majestic river view, but when Jane's folks lived there it was a gracious, private family home.

There was an enormous basement with countless sectioned-off storage and utility rooms. The hallways were uncommonly wide and the rooms were spacious. The dining room was lined with golden oak boisserie and on the landing leading to the second floor was a window seat beneath a mural of richly colored glass. The kitchen managed to be huge and cozy at the same time and there were two pantries adjacent to it. Cars were parked in the carriage house, which had living quarters above it for servants.

It was the attic that I enjoyed exploring the most. It ran the entire length of the house and in every bay there were treasures: Civil War uniforms (Jane's family had fought on the winning side), relics of the Plains Indians, ancient copies of the *National Geographic* all neatly collected, collated, and bundled, copies of *The Saturday Evening Post, Colliers,* and *The Ladies Home Journal,* dusty scenic postal cards from all over the world, a pair of high button shoes, a box of dolls, containers of 78 rpm recordings of Harry Lauter and Caruso, old hats from the turn of the century, old radios that still worked, old umbrellas that didn't, a raccoon coat, a megaphone, antique sleds, and vintage Christmas tree ornaments. It was a storehouse of memories, not just of those who still lived there but of two generations past.

I had never before realized that Davenport was on the banks of the Mississippi. Suddenly there it was in all its broad majesty spread out before me, practically in the front yard.

The river was legendary to me, as fabled as the Amazon or the Ganges or the Nile. I had read about it and flown over it, but I had never been so near it. Visions of Tom Sawyer and Mark Twain and jazz going up river and steamboats and the underground railroad and gigantic catfish raced through my mind. Almost immediately after I arrived I had to go down and put my hands in the water. I felt compelled to feel Mississippi water, to touch it, to be close to it, to know it.

I walked down, plunged my hand into the cold, muddy water, felt the great arterial flow, the throbbing pulse of my country.

It was a solemn and moving moment.

Suspicious stares met me when I returned to the house, for the first contingent of Jane's uncles had arrived. They were staunch Republican, conservative, no-nonsense, Presbyterian, third-generation Scots. They had arrived in time to observe my communication with the great river, and it puzzled them. That, connected with the fact that I was a writer and that I lived in Greenwich Village caused them the greatest concern. Their idea of a writer was Robbie Burns, after which the model has been destroyed. And their conception of Greenwich Village was a place hospitable only to bohemians, practitioners of free love, alcoholic poets, wild-eyed anarchists and Democrats. I was introduced to each of them and they eyed me with caution.

After dinner that evening, the ladies withdrew to the Green Room and the gentlemen went out on the side porch where they lit their cigars. I choked on mine, but I was determined to master it or die in the effort. It soon became clear that the clan had gathered to determine if I was a fit suitor for Jane's hand. It was only with the support and understanding help of Jane's father and her brother, Chuck, that I survived the inquisition.

I remember only one of my responses. It came when Uncle Hugh, the elder of the tribe, said, "I understand you are from an old Virginia family." When I am nervous, I tend to become conspicuously Southern. I was nervous then, and I remember responding in a heavily accented Southern voice: "Yes, sah, we been there about as long as anybody else."

The answer seemed to satisfy the uncles and the conversation turned to coal mining and the advantages of the open-pit method of operation over drilling shafts and delivering the coal to the surface by small-gauge railroad. I chewed on my cigar and nodded as if I understood every word and was going to be given a quiz on it the next day.

During our stay that first time, Jane slept in her old bedroom. It was a charming room. There was a flowered chintz spread on her bed, a window seat, and bay windows with a view of a gazebo that dominated a section of lawn.

There, from the window facing south across the Mississippi, were Illinois and the Rock Island Arsenal. There are moments looking out at the Arsenal that you experience a time warp. You are transported back to when the earliest settlers stopped there and fought Black Hawk for the area, and later to the Civil War where cannons and ammunition were housed along with upward of twelve thousand Confederate prisoners. There are ghosts still there. Even from a distance you can sense their presence.

I was given the guest room near the top of the back stairs. It was a spooky old room, dark even in the daytime, and furnished with antique burled maple pieces that "Faither" had chosen and had sent down from Chicago. I knew the room felt haunted from the minute I entered it. My nervousness grew even greater when I went to bed and found a baseball bat under my pillow. I learned later that it had been kept there ever since 1928 when a burglar had broken in and had gained access to the upper story by way of the adjacent back stairs.

It was midnight when I heard the racket in the hall. I threw on my bathrobe, grabbed the baseball bat, and made my way cautiously into the hall. Jane and Chuck were there and at first I thought they were playing tennis, for they each held tennis rackets aloft, but as I observed them closer I could see that they were chasing something.

"Don't hurt it," Jane warned Chuck.

They were engaged in a nightly ritual they had neglected to tell me about. A family of bats made its home in the attic. After lights out, two or three of them managed to find their way into the upstairs hall. If they were not discouraged, the entire cluster would follow and would spend the night trying to get out through windows and fireplaces. I asked why they had never gassed or poisoned the bats, and Jane looked to me as sternly as one of her uncles and replied that the bats had been there longer than they had. And that seemed sufficient reason for them to be allowed to stay.

Now, Jane and Caroline and Scott and I were back in Iowa. It seemed a haven, an ideal place for Jane and the children to wait while I bravely went on to California, found work, bought a car, and rented a house.

It would have been a great plan if only Aunt Minnie could have been factored out of the equation. Her real name was Jean, and she was Jane's mother's sister. Somehow she had earned the name Minnie Ha-Ha when Jane and Chuck were children. The name had stuck, although no one ever called her that to her face. She was very rich and extremely generous, but she was not easy to live with.

Minnie was what used to be called a "spinster lady." There was supposed to have been a suitor at one time, but nothing had come of it. She had a great fondness for costume jewelry, bright crimson lipstick, and flashy nail polish. She looked like a once-pretty doll that had grown old and now tried to hide the wrinkles with powder. She adored Buicks. Every two years she would buy a new one. She seldom drove her cars. They sat in the carriage house gathering dust, their tires gradually going flat, unless Chuck or Jane happened to be home and would exercise the car or take Minnie for a ride.

Minnie also liked things in their place! Her compulsion went far beyond things being in their normally expected place, such as canned goods in the pantry or umbrellas in the umbrella stand, or plates in a cupboard. For Minnie, each rolled-up window shade had to be at the exact same height from the windowsill that it had always been since she was a child. Each chair in the upstairs hall had to remain in the same spot where it had sat for seventy years. She knew the exact location and condition of every item in the vast attic. Each doll had to be returned to its box exactly so, facing in an exact direction, its arms and legs arranged within a millimeter of where they had been when the doll had been removed. Every book had its exact place on the shelf, no arranged alphabetically, but left exactly where "Faither" had placed it when he finished reading it. Every ancient ba gown, even if it were falling apart, had its own garment ba and coat hanger and position on the clothing rack. Raincoat had to be returned to the hanger from which they had bee removed. Overshoes and galoshes had to be placed in th same spot with mathematical accuracy after they had bee used. Overseeing order in the house was a full-time occupa tion for Minnie.

Several times during the day, Minnie would conduct tour of inspection. She would stalk about the house, he hands resting on the back of her hips, examining each roon critically until she was certain all was well.

If Minnie was unable to return something to its prope place at once, she went into acute melancholia mixed with paranoia. If, for example, a picture frame were slightly askew and too high for her to reach, she would use a broon handle. If that did not work to her satisfaction, she woul send for Mr. Johnson, the gardener, to come and get up on ladder and straighten it. Since Mr. Johnson was well into hi eighties, the danger to him was great, but he was a brav man and he was terrified of Minnie.

Mr. Johnson moonlighted as a minister and his sermon were broadcast on local radio. He never failed to say a spe cial prayer for Jane's family with special emphasis on th hope that "Miss Jean's" soul might be saved. He was espe cially concerned about her use of profanity for if she sent fo him and he was a few minutes late, she would greet him with: "Where in the hell have you been?"

She drove Mr. Johnson equally mad by insisting the grass be mowed in exactly the same pattern, at exactly the same height, on exactly the same day of the week, and that the mowing machine be returned to precisely the same spot in the carriage house where it belonged.

Minnie was also convinced that the house would burn during the night unless every electrical appliance was disconnected. Over the years, with so few people in the house, they had disconnected lamps and appliances that were not in regular use. Still, before she retired at night, Minnie would spend almost an hour disconnecting television sets, lamps, coffeemakers, can openers, everything but the refrigerator. She might have disconnected that, but Jane's mother had drawn the line with the refrigerator.

Minnie was in her seventies when the New York Hamners descended upon her. It was a time of great trial for her. She tried to be a good sport about it, but more often than not she failed.

She felt about the turtle very much the way Donald-R had back at JFK. If the children decided to allow the turtle exercise by giving it the freedom of the upstairs hall, she would stand nearby and warn, "If that thing shits on the floor, I'm not going to clean it up."

"It's okay," the children would assure her. "Mom'll do it."

"They're not supposed to be in the house," she would mutter, then return to her room and close the door until her curiosity would get the better of her and she would be back out monitoring the children again.

The dogs were especially trying to Minnie.

She was always late for meals. Often we would be halfway through breakfast before she came downstairs in the morning.

"I didn't sleep a wink," she would say. "One of those dogs barked all night long."

Actually the cocker spaniels had begun barking again. We attributed it to their being in a strange place and tried to muffle the sound by bedding them down in Jane's closet at night. But Minnie had sensitive ears.

We had tried to train Clem and Chloe when they were younger, but the training had not turned out well. Their barking became a problem to us and for our neighbors, for in New York we lived on the ground floor. Whenever the doorbell would ring for anyone in the building, our dogs would race from the front door to the kitchen screaming as if they were being chased by baboons.

To break them of the habit, I devised an ingenious method. I reasoned that if I could associate the bell ringing with a specific disagreeable experience, it would frighten them into silence. In order to set up this Pavlovian principle, I opened the door to our apartment just slightly, placed several beer cans on top of the door, then went outside and rang the bell.

At the sound of the bell the dogs rushed to the door, screeching at the top of their lungs. Just as they arrived there, I yanked the door open, spilling ten empty beer cans down upon them. They leaped into the air, screeched once, and then ran to the kitchen and hid whimpering under the sink. We were not able to coax them out until the following day.

The experiment worked, but at the same time they began to bark shrilly whenever anyone opened a can of beer. Until the day they died, the sight of a beer can would send them into hysteria. I either had to pour my beer into a glass or take it outside to drink it.

But of the many disruptions we brought to Minnie's life, it was our presence that January that was most distressing to her. Because the weather was extremely cold the amount of time the children could play out of doors was limited, and because they were active and curious young people with inquiring minds they managed to cover the grounds from the most remote and hidden closet in the basement to the furthest reaches of the attic.

Minnie shadowed the children all day long. One day they were exploring in the basement and one of them bumped against an old post hole digger in the gardener's bin. The bump moved it a quarter of an inch. Minnie raced in to place it back to its original position.

Caroline moved an ottoman from in front of a chair to a position closer to the television set. Minnie stood behind her until Caroline got up from the ottoman. Whoosh! The ottoman was back where it "belonged."

When she could take it no longer, Jane turned to me and said, "For God's sake, go to California and find us a place to live!"

The night before I left I thought I was the last one to go to bed. Just to see if she would notice in the morning, when I turned off the television set, I moved the ottoman just an inch or two from its original position. I had turned off the lamp and was starting out of the room when Minnie, who had been lurking in the hall, swooped into the room, righted the ottoman, and stood with her hands on her hips, waiting to see what other disorder I would create before I went to bed. I said goodnight and let the woman finally have some peace.

Jane was right. It was time for us to move on, and I flew out of the Tri-Cities Airport the following day to go to California and look for a place for us to live.

When she learned I was leaving, Minnie took Jane aside and wrote out a generous check in my name.

"He'll never make a living out there in California," she predicted. And for a long time after I arrived here, I wondered how she knew.

6. *Sordid Event on Sunset Strip. Why Hero Had to Leave Sunset Strip!*

My first view of Los Angeles was at twilight. As the plane began its descent, we passed over Lake Arrowhead and then a sparkling expanse of light appeared through a peach-tinted dusk. The plane glided effortlessly over the city and came to rest on the landing strip, a miracle that still never fails to astonish me. I have flown hundreds of thousands of miles, but I am still convinced that flight, other than that accomplished by birds and angels, is illogical and impossible.

Still, to leave behind snowstorms in New York and blizzards in Iowa, to taxi to a safe stop at the end of a runway at LAX, to step out into that wondrously languid evening air and find my friend Russ Landers waiting was a pleasant introduction to Los Angeles.

In Russ's car, he inquired cautiously, "Do you have a job?"

"No," I answered.

"Prospects?" he asked hopefully.

"Not really," I had to admit.

"I hope you brought a little money," he said. "Once they let you in, this town is hospitable. It can even be generous.

Sometimes it can be ridiculous and fun and rewarding and even comfortable, but when you're on the outside, it gives you nothing but a cold shoulder and a slap in the face."

"New York was that way," I observed.

"No," said Russ. "In New York you have only to step off the plane or the train or the bus to become a New Yorker. Here, you have to find a job, 'do' a film, and be invited to a party in Malibu. Until then you're an outsider."

"I've written lots of letters," I boasted, certain that was sure to open the door.

"And you have talent," said Russ cheerfully. "That will count for something."

We drove along streets with names I could not pronounce: La Tijera Boulevard and La Cienega Boulevard. We went through Cahuenga Pass and down streets with the names of canyons that did not look the least like what I thought a canyon should look like.

Russ and his wife, Rosemary, are old friends from Cincinnati. They had invited me to stay with them during those first days in Los Angeles. While Rosemary and I became reacquainted, the Landers children were attracted to the Dobbs hat box that was part of my luggage. Furtive scratching sounds from inside the box suggested that it contained something alive. What was alive there was, of course, Hoaker, the Virginia box turtle that Scott and I had rescued on the road to Richmond.

Some newcomers to California take months or years to adapt to this strange new world. Some never do. They return to the heartland or go back to New York. Often, because they couldn't adapt, they invent stories about our outlandish customs and far-out behavior. Fact is, Californians are strange enough without the exaggeration.

Others adapt right away, and the best adaptation is that which Hoaker and I shared. We stepped off the plane and became Californians. With hardly a backward thought to Virginia, or to his adopted state of New York, Hoaker became a California turtle. As soon as the Landers children discovered he was in the hat box, they insisted on taking him for a walk, and the next time I saw him he was munching contentedly on a dandelion he had appropriated in the Landerses' backyard.

After a weekend with the Landerses, I moved into a small motel on Sunset Boulevard, which I chose for its convenient location. I had to be centrally located since I had no car and would have to take the bus to whatever appointments I could arrange.

Aside from the fact that most of the occupants appeared to be extremely active sexually, it was a homey little place. In the hallway there was a constant parade of couples hurrying toward their rooms. After I had registered and been shown to my room, I became aware of an undulating, syncopated, ceaseless rise and fall of bedsprings that echoed through the courtyard and seemed to come from every room. It could have been this distraction that caused me to overlook the sign that read: NO PETS ALLOWED.

I didn't really consider Hoaker a pet. He was more of a

traveling companion, a refugee, an orphan of that Virginia storm when my son and I had found him, a pioneer in some outlandish relocation scheme that might have him mate with some California desert tortoise and produce a new species that would surely confuse some future Darwin.

But he actually was a pet. We make pets of outlandish companions—snakes, lizards, tigers, dogs, coyotes, guinea pigs, spiders, rabbits, deer, toads, elephants, parrots, cats— whatever animal is available and suits our personalities.

While I was concerned about Hoaker, he didn't give a damn about me. He seemed happiest when he slept his life away, in some dark corner, his head pulled into his shell. The only time he showed even the mildest animation was when I would serve him the tomato and hamburger that were his main diet.

On every floor but mine there were beautiful brown-skinned Mexican chambermaids, many with long braided black hair and merry brown teasing eyes, giggling together over some joke they shared. Many of them had faces that might have been taken from decorations on Mayan temples. They were beautiful to behold and it gave me a warm feeling to hear their giggles as they vacuumed in the lobby.

The happy sounds of giggling were not heard on my floor. My maid was a gaunt, nervous, skittish woman who seemed mostly Mexican but diluted strongly with some other bloodline, quite possibly a descendant of the Mexican line of the Kallakaks and the Jukes. She never smiled, and I'm sure that giggling was totally foreign to her.

I think I was an enigma to her from the very first because I tried with my sophomore University of Richmond Spanish to learn her name. Perhaps none of the other guests had bothered, and it was difficult for her to imagine why it even mattered to me. I was never sure if I was getting through, so I eventually ended up calling her Senorita.

Senorita may have guessed that the turtle was there, for she regarded me with suspicion. Whenever she and I were in the room together, she would position herself so that she might take flight easily. She always made it a point to stay between me and the door.

Some days when she came to clean the room I would be working at my typewriter and would indicate that she could go ahead and clean. She would clean everything in sight without taking an eye away from me, acting for all the world as if I might attack her if she so much as turned her back. As soon as possible she would turn on the vacuum cleaner so as to cut short any attempt at communication and then she would back out of the room cautiously.

Another person who became doubtful of my sanity was the Danish butcher and the Japanese clerk at the market up the street from my motel. Having no car at the time, my marketing was confined to whatever shops I could walk to, and I was delighted when I discovered a small mom-and-pop grocery nearby that boasted a meat department.

I like routine in my life, so at the same time every day I would take my eleven o'clock coffee break and combine it with a trip to the store. At the vegetable counter I would select one tomato and take it to the Japanese woman at the checkout stand. She wore an identification badge with the name Yoko printed on it in pencil.

"This all you want to buy?" Yoko would ask. The look she shot me seemed to suggest that she felt the purchase was hardly worth ringing up.

At first I was tempted to tell Yoko that the tomato was for a Virginia box turtle, but after two or three days, she began looking at me with some anxiety so I decided that any further confidences about my current companion would only induce further distrust.

Following my purchase of the tomato, I would cross to the meat department and ask the butcher to sell me five cents' worth of hamburger.

"You sure that's going to do you?" he asked the first time I placed my order.

"Plenty," I assured him, but the following day when I went back and ordered another nickel's worth of hamburger, I saw him incline his head to his assistant. The assistant came over and stood expectantly beside him.

"You want to give me that order again?" the butcher asked.

"I'll have five cents' worth of your leanest ground round," I said, and saw the butcher give his assistant an "I-told-you-so look."

"Coming right up, sir," he said.

As time passed, I began to notice that on my regular eleven o'clock visit a small crowd would gather ahead of me at the meat counter, small at first, but swelling in number as the weeks went by.

George, the butcher, would come to the counter, look to the crowd and then back to me and say, loud enough to be heard by the crowd, "What can I do for you today, sir?" The people in the crowd would lean forward and then I would repeat my order for five cents' worth of George's leanest ground round. Only when the small ball of ground meat had been weighed, wrapped with a flourish, and paid for did the crowd disperse, and I realized that in a town of extremely odd people, in a part of town that harbors some of its most blatant eccentrics, I had succeeded in becoming one of them!

I had been in the motel only a short time when I arrived back there one morning with my tomato and nickel's worth of hamburger to find a surprise waiting for me in the lobby. All my possessions—my portable typewriter, my suitcase, and my Dobbs hat box with Hoaker in it were packed and waiting for me beside the cashier's desk.

Jose, the young Spanish manager, gazed at me with an aggrieved look as I crossed to his desk.

"What's going on here?" I demanded.

"We do not allow pets," he said accusingly. "It is against the rules."

"You allow everything else," I rejoined. "The bedsprings in this place must have to be replaced every six weeks."

"Your armadillo has attracted ants," he said, "and Estella says she will quit."

"I don't have an armadillo," I said, "and who is Estella?"

"She is your maid and she has fear of you," he said.

I left as graciously as I could under the circumstances, and after a quick glance at the classified section of the *Los Angeles Times*, decided that I had used up Hollywood and there was a nice no-nonsense sound to the name "Studio City."

The cab driver said he knew where it was, and in a moment my "armadillo" and I were headed through Laurel Canyon toward the San Fernando Valley.

7. Hero Rents House from Hell! Saved from Ruin by In-Laws! Enters Twilight Zone!

Shortly after my expulsion from the Sunset Strip, I received a call from Don Congdon. He had arranged with Jim Silberman, a young editor at the Dial Press, to publish *Spencer's Mountain*! A sizable advance against royalties would be forthcoming!

My elation knew no bounds. Not only would I be publishing my second novel—a large hurdle for many writers— would be financially secure for a good long time.

Armed with the promise of an advance, and with most of the money Aunt Minnie had given us, I bought a station wagon and paid the first two months' rent on a house in Studio City, which the owner claimed she had recently renovated. The owner's name was Potter, and since she wore a hat night and day I reasoned that she was either bald or was looking to become a real estate agent. I learned too late that I should have been more cautious.

What a charmer Mrs. Potter was! She assured me that if there were ever a problem, I would only have to shout over the fence because she lived in the house next door and was always available. She picked flowers from her garden and set them on the mantel of the For Rent house so it would not look so empty. While I was considering renting the house, she took me to dinner at a famous Beverly Hills restaurant, and somewhere between cocktails and the after-dinner liqueur, I signed a lease.

The house was a small, one-story bungalow located just off Ventura Boulevard near the local grammar school and within walking distance of shops and markets. Mrs. Potter made such a point of the recent cleanings and renovations that I felt no reservations about paying her several hundred dollars in "cleaning fees" in addition to the two months advance rent and security I had already paid. She assured me that such arrangements were standard. Today I am an informed and aware sophisticate, world famous for my hard heart, known to be a shrewd powerhouse in business and a fox in legal matters, but in those days I was still a good-mannered and trusting Virginian.

Aunt Minnie answered the phone when I called Iowa.

"You need money already?" she asked plaintively.

"Not right yet, Minnie, thanks," I replied.

"You met any movie stars?" she asked.

"I had lunch in the MGM commissary and Gary Cooper was at the next table," I boasted. It was true. As a courtesy to our literary agent, Don Congdon, his client Ray Bradbury had invited me to lunch and Mr. Cooper had indeed been at the next table.

"We've got a place to live!" I told Jane when she came on the phone.

"I'll be right out," she said.

I urged her to stick it out in Iowa just long enough for me to get the house in order and then I would come for her and we could all come back to California together.

Our furniture had already arrived from New York and was being held at a local warehouse. I phoned them and they promised delivery by the end of the week.

I had selected a small quiet room at the back of the house to be my workroom and the day the furniture arrived I could hardly wait for my desk and chair to be set up. The furniture was being delivered by two huge workmen. The one named Herman was stocky and Germanic looking. His hands were the size of shovels but he only used one of them. The other hand held a can of Lowenbrau. His crew cut head reminded me of a novelty plant called Patty O'Hair. The other workman was a smiling Mexican who seemingly spoke no English. Herman called him Manny, which I supposed stood for Manuel.

They struggled in with my rolltop upright desk, which was a valuable, beautifully preserved antique that had been a present from Jane. Next came my swivel chair and finally my typewriter, which had been packed in a wooden case for the journey. Herman and Manny obligingly took the typewriter out of the packing case and placed it on my rolltop desk.

Overjoyed to have everything in place again so that I could get down to the serious business of making a living, I sat down to the typewriter and started to write.

My heart failed me. My "e" did not work, nor did the

shift key, which enables one to capitalize letters. I wrote an indignant note to the shipping company:

    i wish to inform you that th typwritr you shippd m
from nw york has arrivd. vidntally it was injurd in
shipmnt bcaus th lttr that follows d in th alphabt is
no longr working.
    also, i am sad to say that it is no longr possibl
to capitaliz lttrs bcause whn i prss down on th shift
ky it gts stuck and stays stuck. all of this is most
inconvnint sinc i am a writr and mak my living with
my typwritr.
    i hav ownd this typwritr sinc i got out of th
world war 2. thr is a lot of sntimntal valu to it but
i will forgo that if you will simply rplac th machin.
i figur rplacnmt valu is around on hundrd dollars.
    if you rally want to know th truth i'm mad as a wt
hn! plas advis m what you intnd to do in this rgard.

    kindst rgards,
    arl hamnr
    studio city, ca.

The shipping company never acknowledged my letter and I decided to let the matter drop.

I had hardly finished my letter when something shifted under my feet. Very gradually I realized that my desk was beginning to slide ever so gently to the left. Next came a cracking noise and the desk began sliding downward and to the left until it came to rest against the wall. When I knelt down, I discovered that a portion of the floor had crumbled away and that a swarm of winged insects was rising from the hole.

I started out of the house in search of my landlady who lived next door. My exit was barred by the eight-foot sofa, which was supposed to be destined for the living room.

"It's too big," said Herman who was nursing a new can of beer. "We're going to have to bring it in through the window!"

"Do whatever you have to do!" I shouted and rushed out through the back door and called over the fence for Mrs. Potter.

She came at once and I led her into my "office."

"You've brought termites into my house!" she exclaimed when I pointed to the hole in the floor where the insects were still swarming.

"No way!" I shouted. "The floor was already eaten away!"

"They probably came out of that old desk!" she cried.

"The desk hasn't been in the house for more than twenty minutes," I shouted.

"It didn't take long to do its dirty work!" Mrs. Potter complained, and then she leveled an accusatory gaze at me. "This will cost you, you know!"

"But it's not my fault!" I insisted.

There was a polite cough and I turned to see Manny standing just inside the door.

"What is it, Manny?" I asked.

"You come help," he commanded.

Manny led the way to the living room where the window had been removed and the sofa was half in and half out the space where the window had been.

"What have you done to my window?" screamed Mrs. Potter.

"What have you done to her window?" I screamed to Manuel. Manuel shrugged and smiled sweetly.

"Where is Herman?" I screamed.

"*Por favore*, speak slowly the English," said Manuel.

"*Donde es Hermano?*" I screamed in my sophomore Spanish.

"*Beer finito!*" said Manuel sadly. "*Hermano go mas.*"

"When Hermano gets back, tell him he is finito also!" advised Manuel.

At that moment a cab arrived in front of the house and out tumbled three weary travelers and two sickly looking dogs.

"Surprise!" shouted my children. "Surprise!" shouted Jane.

I ran to gather them in my arms. As we moved toward the house, Mrs. Potter advanced toward me, and said, "You didn't tell me there were children!"

"You didn't ask," I said.

"And are those dogs yours, too?" she screeched.

"They are," I said.

"You'll hear from my attorney!" Mrs. Potter called over her shoulder as she went back into her own yard.

Just then Jane cried out, "Why is my sofa sticking out of the window of that little house?"

Jane was a good sport about it when I explained that that "little house" was our new home. Like many pioneer women before her, she moved into what she referred to as "the sod hut" and courageously made the best of it although she started house hunting the very next day.

She was of good cheer even a while later when we went into the living room. Herman and Manny had wrestled the sofa into the room by then. The upholstery had been torn in only a few places and Manny was attempting to cover the torn spots with throw pillows when we entered the room. Once the great sofa was in it, there was barely enough room for anything else.

Herman was standing there and he was just beginning to swill down another beer. He was looking at me with a sweetly sentimental smile as if there were something on his mind and he couldn't decide whether he should say it or not.

"Was there something you wanted to tell me, Herman?" I asked.

He smiled, hiccupped, and then as if confiding a very special secret, he said, "Hitler vas not all bad."

I felt like firing him on the spot but I realized it would leave half of my furniture sitting on the street so I said, "Ja" and encouraged him to go on with his work.

For a short time, California seemed to keep all those promises we had envisioned that previous January when we had watched the Rose Parade on television. The days were sunny, the nights were cool without being cold, rain came only at night—no precipitation ever marred a day. There was only one problem. I had come to Hollywood to work in television and films, but I could not get work.

I had written novels. I had written for radio. I had written segments on *The Today Show*, and I had written live television drama in what is aptly referred to as "The Golden Age." I had even written a parade, for God's sake, the Macy's Thanksgiving Day Parade, to be specific, but it wasn't on film and such was the irrational prejudice at that time that without "something on film" I was not employable in Hollywood!

It was as if there were some mystique about "film" that one had to breathe in with the smog, some secret writing technique that was known to only a few whom the gods had smiled on.

It was Catch-22. I didn't have anything I had written on film and I couldn't get a job writing film until I had some film to show.

What saved us over and over again were checks from the Dial Press and Aunt Minnie, along with suggestions for new directions I might take in my career. At one point, Minnie suggested I go back to college and get a teaching degree.

Finally I remembered that I had once met Rod Serling and that he had taken over the job I had left at WLW in Cincinnati, Ohio, some years earlier. By this time *The Twilight Zone* had become a hit on television. I sent Rod some story ideas by mail and forgot all about them.

We fought the house for our very lives. When it rained there were leaks in every room and we would spend our nights and days placing buckets to catch them. We learned to tread gently, for we would walk down a hallway and a wall would collapse. Overhead soundproofing panels would fall in the middle of the table while we were having dinner. The earth would shift overnight so that the garage door would be jammed shut and we would not be able to use the car.

And then one day the phone rang. The caller was the producer of *The Twilight Zone*, Buck Houghton.

"We like these ideas you sent over," he said. "We want to buy all three."

"I'll have my agent call you," I managed to say.

"We understand you have never written film," said Buck. "Would you like to write them up like little plays?"

"Why don't I write them up like little television film scripts?" I replied.

"Do you think you can do that?" he asked.

"Damned right," I said.

"Go!" said Buck.

I had arrived! My film career was under way. I had made the big break. And it was true that I was never again to want for work in Hollywood.

My good fortune was confusing only to Aunt Minnie. She watched *The Twilight Zone* one evening and became convinced that Rod Serling was "on something" to be capable of writing that kind of stuff, and that I had succumbed to the evils of Hollywood and was "on something," too. Out of pity she continued to send Jane checks and out of consideration for her feelings, we kept them.

When I informed Mrs. Potter that we were moving out of her "sod house" and that I wanted my "fees" returned, she smiled sweetly and said, "Sue me."

8. Simple Pleasures Recalled.
Fowl Deeds on Avocado Drive!

Miracles continued to happen! The *Reader's Digest* bought the condensed book club rights to *Spencer's Mountain*! And then came the most astonishing development of all. Warner Brothers bought the film rights to the novel for a film to star Henry Fonda and Maureen O'Hara.

Suddenly, more money was coming in than a child of the Depression had ever dreamed of making. And it was refreshing for all of us to learn that there was another source of money than Aunt Minnie.

We had rented a small house near the Carpenter Avenue School in Studio City when we first arrived. But now as the lean times passed and we accumulated enough money to make a down payment on a house, we began shopping around.

One of the requirements we had agreed upon was that there be no "Stars" in the neighborhood. We had observed on some of our early house hunting forays in Hollywood that having famous actors for neighbors not only increased the price of real estate, but that one's status depended upon the association. There is a small neighborhood in a residential area called Toluca Lake whose character is almost totally determined by the fact that Bob Hope lives there. People give directions to their house by saying, "It's on the right just three blocks from Hope's house." The resale value of houses on all sides of Mr. Hope's home are nearly doubled in value because they happen to be within aura of Mr. Hope's star.

Stars even shine inappropriately in the educational system. We had shopped for a nursery school for Scott and Caroline and had been offered by more than one school no further enticement than the fact that some prominent actor's children attended that school.

Eventually we settled on a play school for our children. We were momentarily distressed to find that the school mistress had neglected to tell us that in attendance were the children of television star Dennis Weaver. After a bit we discovered that the Weavers were just as eager for privacy as we were, were not out to prove anything, and we relaxed and continued looking for a house to buy.

We were not looking for Avocado Drive. The advertisement we were answering described a house on Laurel Crest Street. We located Laurel Crest Lane, Laurel Crest Road, Laurel Crest Cove, Laurel Crest Drive, but we never did find the street we were looking for. Somehow in the area we became lost and found ourselves on a charming country-like road that wound along the top of a ridge below Mulholland Drive and above Ventura Boulevard. Around every corner we would glimpse views of the floor of the San Fernando Valley stretching across to where the distant ridges of the San Gabriel Mountains rose in a soft blue haze. The houses were neither pretentious nor modest. It seemed a neighborhood of permanence and substance and totally unlike some of the transient neighborhoods we had explored and rejected.

Near the end of the dead-end street we happened to pass a house that caught our attention. It was painted a shade of yellow that the interior decorators might describe as "butter yellow." Mostly it was constructed of glass, framed in wood. There was a brick stairway that led up to the back porch. It was canopied by a noble old walnut tree. The house faced west and was situated high on about a third of an acre of land.

We got out of the car, walked up the driveway and around to the back of the house. There was a neat green lawn. There was a rose garden, a lilac bush, and a small vegetable patch. We looked through the window of what is now our living room. We fell in love, and we still live in that house.

When Jane and I discovered Avocado Drive it was an emotional experience. Something may have spoken to each of us with some meaningful voice from our past. I had been born and nurtured on a hillside in Virginia's Blue Ridge Mountains. Jane had been born in San Diego but she had been raised on a hillside overlooking the Mississippi River in Davenport, Iowa. And now, years later we had come across a landscape that reminded each of us of home. It was per-haps that unconscious recognition of contours and terrain and greenery that made each of us fall in love with the house and the area.

We bought the house and moved into it.

In a short time, our true identities became known. Jane rescued a house sparrow that had been untimely pushed from its nest, named it "Chi-Chi," and fed it peanut butter and ground beef until it had the stamina of an eagle. It survived and flew away, after circling Jane's head in a farewell gesture. She once gave life to a bedraggled bunch of feathers that turned out to be an injured pigeon that never flew again, but was able to stroll around the backyard, and was known for the rest of its life as "Yard Bird." Jane once attempted to keep three baby squirrels alive when they had been swept from their nest in a windstorm, only to find too late that they needed to be taught to urinate. She once brought back to life three infant guinea pigs named "Yankee," "Doodle," and "Dandy." For these reasons, Jane became known in the neighborhood as something of a miracle worker. The owner of any injured pet found his or her way to our house, where more often than not, Jane sent the injured or dying patient on its way alive or recovering.

After a while, she became known as "The Bird Lady," and I became known as "The Bird Lady's Husband"!

We were blessed with good neighbors on Avocado Drive. Scott and Caroline had gangs of other children to play with. The animals had ample room in which to roam, and with a few exceptions the benign sun shone with almost monotonous regularity. What this Paradise lacked, I decided, was a sense of continuity, customs that could be handed down from one generation to another, something from my past that I might will to my children.

When I was a boy in Virginia during the Great Depression we amused ourselves as inexpensively as possible. Pleasure was catching minnows in Witt's Creek. Joy was the beginning of summer when we were finally freed of shoes and could savor the sheer delight of running barefoot again. Ecstasy was a Sunday afternoon visit to Uncle Benny Tapscott's farm in Buckingham County where the ripe watermelon had been cooling in the spring for two days. Uncle Benny Tapscott would slice generous helpings of the cold red melon. We would gorge ourselves, tossing the rinds in the weeds, spitting the seed on the ground until our bellies became distended and our voices raspy from singing "Let Me Call You Sweetheart" and "Down By the Old Mill Stream."

Some evenings after supper was over, the dishes washed, and the homework finished, the family would listen to the radio. We would sit somewhat formally in the living room, staring at the green light on the old Atwater-Kent table model radio while Jack Benny and Mary Livingston shared tales of Jack's miserliness and her adventures as a clerk at The May Co. Fred Allen led us down Allen's Alley where we met the likes of Senator Claghorn and Minerva Pious. George Burns was telling much the same jokes he told to his dying day. We were convulsed when the door to Fibber and Molly McGee's closet was opened, spilling its contents thunderously into the living room. By the time "One Man's Family" came on, we youngsters were packed off to bed to leave our parents to ponder the trials and tribulations of the Barbours.

Some evenings, my father would decide that we were running up too exorbitant an electric bill and he would decree that we would not use the radio. On such an evening we would sit on the front porch and share with my father a mystical experience. He would give a signal and my four brothers, my three sisters, my mother, and I would fall silent.

He would then begin a series of whistling sounds which were an incredibly accurate reproduction of the call of the male bobwhite quail. "Bob-white! Bob-white! Bob-white!" Silence. And then far off in the distance, across the crab apple orchard, across Drusilla's Pond, across the dark field of evergreens behind the Baptist Church, would come the answering call of the bobwhite hen.

We children would shiver with excitement. Our father was communicating with something wild, summoning it out of the wilderness into our lives and experience.

If we kept silent, the bird could be coaxed through the falling darkness to the very edge of the yard, and when she discovered she had been lured by a false lover, she would take off with an explosive lift of her wings and disappear into the darkening sky.

What I needed, I finally decided, to make Avocado Drive complete was the presence of bobwhite quail. I dreamed of sitting on the porch at night and summoning the birds from the fields. I would astonish my children as my father had astonished me and call wild quail in from the darkness. I was determined to correct what I considered an imbalance in nature. If there were no bobwhite quail in California, then I would import them.

I found an advertisement for a game bird farm in the western San Fernando Valley. It was a ramshackle farm located behind a modest frame house. The "farm" consisted of several long wire enclosures in which there were exotic birds I had never even imagined encountering in the San Fernando Valley. Pheasants from India, grouse from Scotland, peafowl from England, Japanese chickens with long flowing tails, African guinea fowl, and yes, some bobwhite quail.

I heard the slap of a screen door and turned to see the owner coming my way. She was a woman in her sixties wearing bleached overalls that covered what appeared to be a blue Brooks Brothers oxford cloth shirt and a beaked cap that advertised the Hitchcock film *The Birds*.

"Where you from, honey?" she demanded.

"Virginia," I said.

"I mean, what production company?" she said.

I explained that I was not with a production company, which seemed to disappoint her, for it turned out that the bulk of her business came from supplying trained birds to movie and television studios. When I explained that I wanted to buy some bobwhite quail eggs and the reason for buying them, she was most helpful.

"If you want to colonize them, you'll have to hatch them where you want them to stay. Where do you live?"

"Studio City," I told her.

"I don't think Studio City is the best place to raise quail," she said. "But let's give it a try."

She explained that if the quail were born in the area they might tend to stay there, so it would be best to hatch and raise them somewhere near the house. In the end, she sold me a dozen quail eggs and a small bantam hen. She instructed me to make a nest and place the eggs in it and she swore that the hen would become broody, sit on the eggs, and hatch them.

I built a handsome nest of straw and placed the eggs in the center. The hen ignored the eggs and the nest. One thing that may have turned off the hen was that I did all the work. She had no pride of ownership because I built the nest. I hovered over the eggs. I dug up the fat worms that lived in my garden and brought them to her as a bribe.

The hen ignored the luxurious nest. She ignored the quail eggs, but she did consent to eat the night crawlers. Hoping to persuade her to begin mothering the quail eggs before they spoiled, I reasoned that she was leading an unnatural life. She was a single chicken living all alone. How could I expect her to perform a responsible family function if she did not belong to a family?

I went back to the bird farm and purchased a rooster. He was a bantam rooster, a bird of great beauty in colors of black and brown and russet and red and yellow. He was a thing of such strutting radiance that he might have been designed by an artist. He knew he was a handsome thing and he told everybody in the neighborhood about it—each morning at around five o'clock.

"I am handsome," his crowing would seem to say. "I am beyond compare in the richness of my feathers, my stately bearing, and my lordliness. I am the cock of the walk!"

The little hen seemed to adore him. During his crowing sprees, she would walk about scratching industriously with first one foot and then the other, feeding on the seed she uncovered, and clucking appreciatively.

The rooster would start crowing as early as five o'clock and continue well into the morning. The neighbors on Avocado Drive realized soon after we had moved in that we were not your run-of-the-mill Hollywood types. Many of them were tolerant, but not all of them.

At first I would go down to the chicken pen and shoosh the rooster. He would remain quiet for a while, probably shocked into insensibility at the sight of me. I am told by those who have seen me that at that hour of morning I resemble an enraged ostrich. But as time passed, my entreaties did nothing to quiet the unruly monster.

Repercussions were not long in coming. It was not yet first light. The house was still with that special quiet when the only sound is the river of sleep

that flows from quiet room to quiet room. I became con
scious that the phone was ringing and I reached for it with
a sleep-drugged hello.

"This is Dusty Rhyder," the aggrieved voice said. "I live
up the street from you."

"Yes, Mr. Rhyder?" I said, becoming instantly awake.
knew from past experience that Mr. Rhyder would take hi
grievances all the way to the governor of the state if he di
not receive satisfaction.

By day he was a stern, uniformed, bureaucratic officia
with the Department of Animal Regulations. For almost
year, we had to hide one of our dogs from him because w
were over the legal limit, and we knew he would not hes
tate to report us to his superiors. By night, he was somethin
else. At first when he emerged from his garage in th
evenings, we did not recognize him. He drove a re
Trans-Am convertible with steer horns adorning the from
grille, and he was dressed like a cowboy. Mr. Rhyder
bumper sticker read: "Cowboys Do It Better."

Mr. Rhyder adored cowgirls and evidently they adore
him right back. He brought them home at all hours of th
night and sometimes they would arrive on their own. I
almost every case they were dressed in fringed jackets, shor
short skirts, and calf-length boots. If he did not admit ther
at once they would beat on his gate or pound their car horr
until he came to the gate to let them in. Country and wes
ern music would have the neighborhood throbbing unt
well after midnight.

And now Mr. Rhyder was on the phone and he was complaining to me!

"I work at night," Mr. Rhyder complained, "and I need my morning sleep."

"How can I help you?" I asked.

"It's your rooster," he said. "It's crowing again!"

"I'm sorry," I said, "but you know, that rooster is a watch-rooster! It crows whenever there's a prowler in the neighborhood."

"Don't give me that bull," said Mr. Rhyder. "It starts crowing every morning at five o'clock on the dot."

He was dead right, but I thought I would push my luck.

"It just so happened that I saw a prowler near your house just a few minutes before you called," I lied. "That rooster is on guard and doing a damn good job."

"What did the prowler look like?" asked Mr. Rhyder.

"She was dressed in a cowgirl costume," I lied. "And she was trying to get through your gate."

"I'd better take a look," replied Mr. Rhyder, and he hung up the phone.

I attempted to get back to sleep, trying to ignore the fact that the rooster was indeed awake and crowing stridently. I began to half believe my story about his being a watch-rooster when the phone rang again.

"Dusty Rhyder here!" the voice said.

"Yes, Mr. Rhyder?"

"I think you were pulling my leg," he said.

"Oh," I objected, "I would never do that."

"I looked, and there wasn't any prowler. I know you're a writer and have an imagination, and I think you just made that story up."

"Oh, I would never do something like that," I said.

"I'm going to report you in the morning," he said and hung up the phone.

I struggled out of bed, found my bathrobe, and made the long journey down to the chicken pen. The rooster was perched as high as he could get and singing lustily. The hen was perched beside him and it appeared to me that he was singing just for her. The rooster paused in his concert long enough to look at me inquiringly, and then began anew his raucous greeting to the dawn.

I tucked him under my arm and went to the garage where I found an empty corrugated cardboard box. Enclosed in the darkness, the rooster fell silent and I returned to bed.

This procedure worked so well that I faithfully tended to the chore each night before retiring. On occasion I would have to attend an award ceremony such as the Oscars or Emmys, but even in black tie, I would make my way down to the poultry compound, catch the rooster, and place him in his box for the night. I bet I was the only writer in Hollywood whose tuxedo had bird stains on it. The dry cleaner I went to, and still do business with, has never inquired as to why, and I have never volunteered any information. As far as they are concerned we are good customers, for we soil a lot of clothes and we always pay our bills on time.

For all the trouble he caused me, the rooster still did not produce the results I looked for in the little family I had put together. Rather than becoming broody and mothering the quail eggs I had provided, the hen began laying her own eggs and ignoring the quail eggs.

At this point I reasoned that fowl do not function as a family, but as a flock, and that what I needed to establish a normal routine in the chicken pen was another hen.

I brought her home, a jaunty, independent little thing. She had sharp intelligent eyes and a quick jerky walk. She immediately explored her new home and she seemed delighted with her surroundings even after First Hen established her dominance by nearly pecking her to death.

But Second Hen, however dominated, found an interesting revenge. Whenever First Hen left her nest, Second Hen would rush in and steal her eggs and send them careening around the pen with her foot as if they were bowling balls. First Hen would then collect her eggs back again and march back and forth as if daring Second Hen to come near them.

One evening when I came home from work, Scott met me with the news that First Hen was acting "funny."

"Funny how?" I asked.

"Her feathers are all fluffed out and she tries to peck you if you go near her," he answered.

"That's a sign she's broody," I said. "She's ready to hatch eggs."

We hurried down to the chicken pen and found First Hen already on the nest, scrunched down protectively over an empty nest. Scott and I found the quail eggs, which had somehow gotten shunted to a corner and placed them under her. She made low threatening noises in her throat, but being an old country boy I recognized them as further evidence that she was truly ready to hatch eggs and raise a brood.

Scott and I could hardly wait for the next morning. Right after breakfast we visited the chicken pen but we were met with disappointment. During the night First Hen had rejected the quail eggs. They had been rolled out of the nest and most of them were broken.

"Why don't we put the chicken eggs under her?" asked Scott.

"Because they wouldn't hatch," I said. "They've been scrambled because they've been tossed around so much."

"I'd like to try it anyway," said Scott.

"They won't hatch," I said.

Scott gave me his oh-ye-of-little-faith look, gathered up all the scattered chicken eggs in the pen and placed them under First Hen.

She huddled down and began to cluck contentedly. In a few days she went into a trance and barely moved. I kept trying to find some way to soften the blow for Scott when the day came that we would have to remove the eggs from under First Hen. They were sure to be rotten.

About three weeks later, I had just sat down to breakfast when I heard Scott shouting out by the chicken pen. Jane, Caroline, and I went running.

Lurching about the pen, pecking hungrily and preening

with what surely must have been pride was First Hen. Following her were twelve of the most beautiful chicks imaginable. They looked like decorations for Easter baskets—healthy, inquisitive, hungry little black and yellow balls of fluff. They careened around the pen until their mother's cluck would call them back to her. Then they would huddle under her feathers until she gave them permission to venture forth again.

Scott was kind enough not to say, "I told you so."

One of the brood he named Blackie, an exceptionally bright chicken who enjoyed extraordinary longevity.

I was glad for Scott that his faith had paid off. I was glad for First Hen that she had a brood of chicks. But I must honestly say that I felt cheated.

That covey of bobwhite quail I had dreamed of for my hill had still not materialized. But I didn't give up! I sent away for something called a "Quail Kit," but that is another story.

9. Unsavory Elements in the Garden!

"Her name is Susie Green," said Caroline. She held up a Mason jar with something in it for my inspection.

"What is it?" I asked. I could see only a few blades of grass and a lettuce leaf in the bottom of the jar.

"Right there," said Caroline. And she pointed to the lettuce leaf. When I looked more closely, I spotted a tiny, garden-variety snail.

"Isn't she beautiful!" said Caroline, and when I looked more closely I had to admit that she was right.

The snail was the size of a pea. Its spiral shell was patterned in pale gray and faint yellowish brown, and it was moving itself gently across the lettuce leaf, leaving behind a glistening trail of slime. From its snout extended two feelers, which would retract or extend themselves as the snail encountered barriers or open country. Directly below each feeler were tiny dots, quite possibly eyes, on stalks. Because of its youth, its shell was almost transparent, so delicate that the slightest pressure could crush and kill it.

Only Caroline would find beauty in something other people would overlook or find ordinary. She was always sensitive to people and to her surroundings and observed them poetically. Once when some fog clouds hung low over the San Gabriel Mountains she observed, "The mountains have little dreams on them."

Now that a snail had become a part of the family, so to speak, I had a problem. I could not with good conscience feed Susie Green a cabbage leaf, then go out in the garden and wantonly step on one of her relatives. To poison one of her brothers or sisters seemed equally reprehensible. There is a substance in the snail "bait," as it is called, which lures snails to it. Once they eat the pellets, their flesh liquifies and bubbles up out of their shells. From what I have been able to tell, death does not come quickly.

But the snail problem was a real one. I had planted a garden of tender and succulent vegetables, just the kind of fodder the little devils love to graze on. Not only do they multiply by laying millions of eggs, which hatch in twenty-two days; they are clever at hiding under rocks, boards, grass, in cracks, or the underside of plants—anywhere that is moist and dark. Even if you eliminate every snail from your property, they will migrate from other people's yards. I even tried handpicking them once and dropping them into the yard of one of my neighbors who is a pest, but they came right back. They seemed to prefer my garden to his. Some people eat snails, and I have myself, but having had an escargot in the family, I can no longer eat them.

The problem was intensified when Caroline decided that Susie Green was not happy in her jar and resolved to give her her freedom.

The film *Born Free* was popular at the time. Caroline loved it and, taking a clue from the movie, she released Susie Green to the wilds for short periods of time so Susie could gradually become accustomed to freedom, just as Joy Adamson had done with Elsa the lioness.

I became resigned to turning the entire garden over to Susie Green and her family. Let them eat my evergreens, digest my dahlias, consume my cosmos, destroy my delphinium, and munch on my marigolds. As much as I pretended I didn't care, I did. I cared a great deal.

The problem was solved with amazing ease. I believe I read it in *Sunset Magazine*, in an article about acceptable ways to cope with the pesky things.

Following Sunset's directions, I set out several deep-dish pie pans half filled with Bud Light. In the morning, a half dozen big fat fellows were floating in each of the pie pans. In the days that followed, I found snails of all sizes in their oozy grave.

The snail population diminished, but it never reached zero. There was always the occasional individual that either eluded my trap or had just recently arrived from somebody else's yard. But with so few present, the damage to my crops and my ornamental plants was light, and I learned I could live with it.

Only when she reads this will Caroline learn that I probably drowned Susie Green in beer. She herself is a gardener of note with a very special interest in horticulture, and I have the feeling that she will understand and forgive me.

10. Hero Reflects at Length on the Sport of Fishing and Relationships Between Fathers and Sons!

ishing is an ancient and traditional pursuit, probably the most democratic of sports. It is as available and as enjoyable o a small boy with a bent pin tied to a piece of string as it is o the sportsman who has chartered a boat to troll for marin in the Florida Keys.

It is above all a companionable sport. Screaming fans, blessing and cursing their favorites on a baseball diamond, may provide some basic companionship to those present. But eep basic companionship can exist between two people who are fishing together. Sometimes they can even be at a istance from each other. I have spent an entire day casting a ly toward a golden trout native on the Kern River without nowing a soul I passed, but felt a closeness and kinship with he man exploring the adjoining pool although our commuication might consist of a nod or a "How ya doin'?" And the esponse might be anything from a despondent grunt to a etailed description of the capture of the splendid specimen e will exhibit with the slightest encouragement.

Perhaps it is the companionship that makes most fishing fathers look forward with the keenest anticipation to the first time they can share the sport with their sons.

For my son, Scott, and me that time came not long after we had moved from New York City to California. I began doing research soon after we arrived and determined that our best chance for a productive fishing expedition might be at Lake Cachuma, a reservoir in the Santa Ynez Mountains not far from Santa Barbara.

To make the expedition even more exciting, we decided to stay overnight at nearby Solvang. Solvang is a Danish gathering just inland from Santa Barbara. Today it has taken on the commercial appearance of any number of "theme parks," but in those days it boasted two motels, a sleepy and charming little main street, and a windmill that housed a bakery. And it had the near-genuine personality of a small Danish village.

Jane and Caroline said good-bye to us with a remarkable lack of emotion. Thus Scott and I were introduced to the fact that women enjoy each other's company, and the females of our household were indeed looking forward to spending the entire weekend without us.

I have forgotten what Scott and I discussed on our way to Solvang. I expect I pontificated, and I am sure I glorified and sentimentalized fishing to a degree that no reality could ever measure up to. Knowing me, I probably even made extravagant promises as to the number and size and ferocity of the fish we would catch once we were on the lake.

I know I did not tell Scott one fishing story that I always remember with a certain amount of pain, but I will tell it to him now:

Fishing was the one activity my father and I were able to enjoy together without reservation. My father and I had some reservations about each other: I was an odd child with a vivid imagination. He found my imagination discomforting. It made him uneasy to see me pulling a small wooden wagon that to my mind was filled with eleven black and white English setter puppies. I knew their parentage, their individual dispositions, their names, and what was going to become of each of them.

In truth, the wagon was empty, and so it appeared to my father. It was difficult for him to see the puppies I saw there. He would look at me and I could see the concern in his eyes. But I saw puppies, and could not be convinced that they were not there.

In spite of his discomfort with me, he would still take me fishing. I suppose these adventures were intended to check up on how far my "oddness" had progressed, for he would look anxiously and quickly at anything I pointed out to see if indeed the thing were there and visible. I remember pointing out a painted turtle floating on the surface of Drusilla's Pond and my distress when it sounded and disappeared totally from view before my father could spot it. Fortunately, it left an expanding circle on the surface in its wake, so he at least gave me the benefit of the doubt.

Usually we would go fishing on Drusilla's Pond in the

evenings after my father had finished work. Two of my second cousins had drowned there, caught in the roots of trees when they dived in a secret and furtive frolic to cool off from a hot August afternoon. Their names were Arlene Giannini and Eddie Dean, and even today when I linger as the first shadows fall across the pond at night, I can see their ghosts silently hovering on the opposite side of the pond. Their images ripple as the evening breeze disturbs the surface of the water. When I was a boy I fancied they beckoned me to come to them to save their lives and to bring them to the surface and to life again. I did not tell my father. Today I still see them, but I know that I cannot give them life except to record that they lived, the place where they died, and their sweet and faded memories.

Fishing on Drusilla's Pond was recreational and instructive. We fished for fun, and if we caught anything at all it would be one of the brilliantly colored "sunfish," which was the name we gave to the perch. Still it was practice for the future, the way station before we graduated to big water. It was a learning pond. Once we had learned the lessons of the pond we became qualified to fish the Rockfish River.

The Rockfish has its headwaters up around Crabtree Falls in the highlands of Nelson County, Virginia. In its mountainous region the stream holds trout, but as it meanders off through level country the water warms up, leaving the trout behind and picking up smallmouth bass, crappie, garfish, eels, suckers, catfish, and carp.

The Rockfish flows into the James at the Howardsville

Bridge. During the old days it was the place where the fur trap-pers from the mountains met the flatboats ferrying tobacco and furs down to Richmond and Jamestown and Williamsburg.

My father's favorite fishing spot was on a rock below the dam at Howardsville. It was a private place, difficult to find and to get to. I don't think he shared it with anyone except his sons. The rock was just off a point that jutted out into the river. When the water level was low, one could walk there on a series of steppingstones without even getting one's feet wet. If the water level was normal and the current swift, wading out to the rock could be a formidable undertaking.

The first time my father took me out to the rock I was just a little boy and he carried me in his arms through the swift current. I held the poles and the bait and the beer. He held me. I will never forget the strength of his arms, the secure feeling I had, and the sense of adventure of crossing dangerous water to reach a firm and treasured piece of earth.

We caught bass and catfish that day, the two of us com-fortably sitting back against the rock. My father let me taste the beer several times and we both got clobbered.

Drink made my father verbose and we almost forgot about the fishing as he went on a storytelling binge. One story followed another, stories of his exploits as a hunter and fisherman. He told stories of the poverty he had known as a boy, of a rattlesnake "as big around as a lumberjack's leg" he had killed, and of the mysteries that still lurked back in the mountains.

The last time we went to that special place was in 1968.

It was autumn and the fishing season was almost over and there was small chance that we would catch anything. Still, my father wanted to go there and I did, too.

My father was ill. He had always seemed outsized to me, braver and stronger than any other man, invincible, larger than life. On this visit home I was shocked that the man I remembered weighing one hundred and eighty pounds had withered away to a hundred and ten. The same devilish smile was there in the gaunt face, but for the first time I saw fear there, too, and felt fear myself, for soon after I arrived home he told me he did not have long to live.

It was not until we reached the edge of the water and were faced with crossing to the rock that I realized how the tables had turned. This time it was I who would carry my father, and it was he who carried the bait, the beer, and the poles.

Once we were settled on the rock my father did not fish. He tossed out a line, but he let it go slack or he allowed the bait to wander wherever it wanted to go. His mind was not on fishing. He seemed more intent on passing on to me all those things he felt he might never have a chance to say again.

"Don't ever get in red ink, son," he said. "You'll spend your life trying to get out."

My father had recently paid off the loan he had taken on our house. It was his—finally. He owned it, and he was proud of that, but I remembered all the years he had been in "red ink" and how it had distressed him to be indebted to another man.

After this advice he sat for a while, thinking and staring off down the river. Then after a moment he said, "Don't run with bad women. They'll ruin your life."

The fact that I was already married to a good woman seemed to have escaped him. Perhaps he was suggesting that "bad women" were a continuing threat, even to a married man, and I wondered what temptations might have put themselves in his way during those many years he had worked away from home and could only be with his family on weekends.

His final bit of advice was: "Look every man straight in the eye." By this time we were both drowsy from the beer and the sunshine, and we simply enjoyed being together and the flow and drift and sparkle of the river around the rock we rested on. Finally I caught an eel, which made my line slimy in its twisting, frantic attempt to escape.

I cut the line, lifted my father back to the river bank and we returned home. The next time I saw him he was dead, and the eyes that had looked straight at every man were closed forever.

The memory of my last fishing trip with my father stayed with me during my first fishing trip with my son.

We checked in at the St. George Motel in Solvang and went immediately out to the lake. It was a bad day for fishing. A strong wind had come up, and the concessionaire would not allow us to rent a boat.

We walked along the lakefront until we came to a likely looking spot. Empty cigarette packages, used candy wrappers, and discarded lure containers told us that other fisher-men had used the spot before. It gave promise that we, too, might catch fish. We fished there without success until darkness fell.

We slept soundly at the motel and were back on the lake at sunup. The boat concession had not even bothered to open that day because the wind was still dangerously high out on the lake.

Scott was a patient, intent, serious fisherman. He held his rod alert, as if he expected a bite at any second. Even when lunchtime arrived and I suggested we go into town  for a snack, he insisted we remain and catch the fish I had promised him.

Finally the bite came! It was not a spectacular bite, but there was a fish on the line and the first action we had seen the entire weekend.

Scott played the fish for a moment, and with me holding my breath, and trying to stay quiet for once, he brought to shore a three-inch-long crappie. And there was a look in Scott's eyes that was worth the long and trying wait.

After he had examined the fish, Scott said, "Let's go home."

I thought that was a good idea, but I urged him to release the crappie and let it grow, but it was the first fish he had ever caught and he wanted to take it home and show it to his mother and sister.

"It won't be in much shape to show anybody by the time we get it home," I said.

"Sure it will," answered Scott. "I'm going to keep it alive."

I geared myself to help Scott face one of the facts of life. "It's out of its element. We have a two-hour trip home and we have nothing to carry it in. It will die."

Scott gave me his "oh-ye-of-little-faith" look and scouted along the edge of the lake until he found a rusting old coffee can that had once held night crawlers. He filled it with water. The crappie had been swimming around, the hook still embedded in its mouth. Scott took the crappie out of the water and together we removed the hook, which had done no great damage. Once in the coffee can, the crappie gave us a malevolent look then sank to the bottom where I was convinced he would die before we had gone five miles down the highway.

Scott had filled the can to the brink with water and scolded me for driving recklessly each time an ounce or two of the water spilled from the can.

We soon discovered that my reckless driving was not the only cause of the rapidly falling water level. The coffee can had developed a leak—or maybe it had been there all along—whichever the case, it now seemed to be growing minute by minute. We had come as far as Oxnard when Scott said, "We've got to find something else to put this fish in. We're running low on water."

We were on the freeway and nowhere near any house or place of business where a new container could be found. I increased my speed but by the time we reached an exit large enough to boast a filling station, the water had almost completely drained out of the can and the crappie was flopping about in desperation.

I braked in front of the filling station and ran inside to ask the attendant for a container of some kind.

"I'm trying to keep this fish alive," I explained.

"I don't see any fish," he answered, looking at me warily.

"He's out in the car flopping around," I said. "The coffee can had a hole in it."

The more I explained, the more I seemed to confuse the attendant. Finally he began looking around the station for an empty container, but he could find nothing. Realizing I was wasting time, I dashed outside and crossed to the car. Scott and the fish had vanished.

I decided that the fish had died and that Scott was tearful and, not wishing to be embarrassed, he had gone behind the filling station for privacy.

I did find Scott behind the station, but he wasn't in tears nor was the fish dead. He had found a used milk carton in a garbage heap and had filled it with water from the tap in the restroom. The crappie now rested in what I was sure was its grave. The water was the color of skim milk. Tap water contains chlorine, which is usually fatal to fish. Surely, I thought, the crappie's merciful end will come somewhere between here and home.

All conversation between Scott and me ceased. I drove as fast as I dared. We were in a race with time and neither of us felt a need to mention it. We sat, grim-faced and silent, until we reached home.

Caroline and Jane met us with eager inquiries about the catch. Scott proudly displayed the milk carton. We rushed to his room where he emptied the contents of the carton into his aquarium.

The aquarium was a twenty-gallon tank. It contained an established colony of tropical freshwater fish, most of them live bearers, all of them treasured old friends. The guppies were the result of a long, selective breeding program by which Scott had developed a variety with extraordinarily long flowing tails, each of them tinged with a nearly solid golden tail. Black mollies abounded and some swordtails and ghost catfish with bodies so transparent you could clearly view their respiratory and digestive systems functioning.

It was a waterscape Scott had tended carefully, a vista where a porcelain castle looked out over waving fields of sea grass. A sunken treasure chest half submerged in the sand spilled out gold and silver coins. A deep-sea diver lowered himself on a cable directly over the treasure and in the corner, half submerged, a Spanish galleon rested on its rotting hull.

For a little while after the milk carton and its contents went into the aquarium, the water turned a pale milky color. Gradually the water became clear. At first there was no sign of the crappie.

We located him finally, sullenly hiding between the ribs of the Spanish galleon. He appeared loggy and not the least bit well. Sporadically he would make a run to the top of the water as if to gulp in oxygen, and then he would dash back to his hiding place in the ribs of the Spanish galleon.

I worried about what might ail the crappie now. He had survived suffocation from being out of water, and he had survived submersion in a mixture of milk and chlorinated tap water. What if this final change of temperature had been too much for him? Ordinarily when you transfer a live fish from one environment to another, care must be taken that the temperature of both habitats are the same. Usually you accomplish this by floating the fish in a plastic bag in the aquarium for ten or fifteen minutes while the temperature of the water in the bag is raised or lowered to match the temperature of the water outside the bag.

I resisted the temptation to warn Scott that the fish might not last the night. He had already proved me wrong too many times that day. I did however advise him that the crappie might pass a less troubled night if the fluorescent light in the tank were turned off to let its citizens get a good night's sleep.

We all slept soundly until dawn when a great shout of anger and grief came from Scott's room.

We rushed there to find Scott peering with dismay into the aquarium. The crappie was prowling around the tank like a miniature shark. There was one solitary guppy left and even as we watched, it swam languidly out from the protection o the castle and was devoured. There was not a single tropical fish left. The seascape with its castle and fields of sea grass was plowed and uneven, evidence of the struggle the tame fish had put up in a vain effort to save their lives.

Scott kept the crappie for several days, but he never developed the fondness for it that he felt for the tropical fish the crappie had cannibalized. Eventually he released the wild fish into the Tujunga Creek.

Generational events have a way of repeating themselves. I doubt that my last fishing expedition with Scott will end with his lifting me over to my favorite rock, as happened with my father and me. Still, it may be that some day after he has become the grownup and I have become the child, that it will be I who tries to bring home my catch in a leaky coffee can.

11. Caught in Charlotte's Web!

All my life I have felt a kinship with every living creature. It pains me to go to a zoo and see animals caged. I am the original "tree hugger," and I have never gotten over the sick feeling that came over me when I accidentally kicked a pigeon in Central Park.

That regard somehow never extended to spiders. I cannot ever remember being afraid of them. On the other hand I had no particular liking for them. If I came in contact with one I usually dealt with it by swatting it with whatever might be at hand.

Through my writing my relationship with spiders changed, and I was never in my life to see or think of one in quite the same way again.

It was a plum of an assignment. I was chosen to write the film script for Hanna-Barbera's animated version of E. B. White's classic tale, *Charlotte's Web*.

Mr. White was an idol. I knew his work from his pieces in *The New Yorker* and his children's book *Stuart Little*. As a writer with serious goals I kept a copy of *The Elements of Style*, the book White edited and cowrote with William

Strunk Jr. As a young writer who had come to New York in the 1950s I knew almost by heart every word of his famous essay "Here Is New York," which had originally been published in a single issue of *Holiday Magazine*.

And now I was being given the opportunity to dramatize one of White's most beloved works. I remember saying facetiously to my agent that I would write the film script without a fee. The agent was shocked beyond words that his client might even consider working for no pay and sternly admonished me never to say such a thing again.

But it was not the fee that thrilled me. It was the pleasure of working with Mr. White's words and story.

In doing my research I learned a great deal about spiders. They even earned my grudging admiration if not my respect. I learned that they have special appendages called spinnerets with which they spin the silk to make their webs. While I had been aware of the common house spider I learned that there are about three thousand different kinds of spiders in our country alone. They have such exotic names as fishing spiders, wolf spiders, goldenrod spiders, as well as one with the fascinating name elongated long-jawed crab! I learned that a tarantula is a spider. A daddy longlegs is not!

Charlotte is actually Charlotte Cavatica who befriends Wilbur the pig when he comes to live in the barnyard. Wilbur is naturally bereft when he learns that his destiny is to be killed and made into sausage and bacon. Charlotte pledges to try to save Wilbur's life. She does so by writing a series of messages in her webs.

It is a marvelous story of miracles, of birth and death, of threat and hope and courage and friendship and regeneration. And on top of all its many other qualities it is funny. Templeton the rat, with his selfish outlook on life and love of garbage, is a howl.

During the writing of the script I came to have the highest regard for Charlotte. The messages she writes in her web are clever and insightful and effective. She saves Wilbur's life, but she cannot save her own. When she is near death she explains what friendship means, and through her death E. B. White shows us the magic of life regenerating itself.

I remember coming near the writing of the end of the story. Ordinarily I try to remain objective from the scene I'm writing. Even in a scene of high drama I try not to become emotionally involved, but in the final pages of the book Charlotte is near death. As I was writing the scene my phone rang. The caller said, "You sound all choked up. Is something wrong?"

I replied, "Yes, a spider just died."

My empathy with spiders became more pronounced once I saw the completed film. Debbie Reynolds supplied the voice of Charlotte. The outrageous comedian Paul Lynde played Templeton the rat, and Henry Gibson furnished the voice of Wilbur the pig. And in the role of the double-talking goose we were able to hire the distinguished actress Agnes Moorehead. And to top it all off the musical score by Bob and Dick Sherman gave the entire production deep and memorable moments that only music can supply.

The film did modest business in the theaters, but on videocassette it achieved real success. It was and still is a bestseller. Many parents tell me that their youngsters watch the tape at least once a week and are spellbound each time. To my delight I have become a hero to the preschool set! It is a responsibility!

In late summer here in California the spiders known as orb weavers come to town. They are small guys at first, but they are experts at building large webs and as they feed on their numerous victims they quickly grow enormously fat. They are not unattractive spiders. Ours are the color of brick and they have nice-looking black and brown banded legs.

They are an industrious crowd. They seem to build a new web overnight. At first you are unaware and then one morning you walk out and your face and hair are enmeshed in a web that was built overnight. My first tendency was to tear the damn thing down, and then I would hear Charlotte's voice telling Wilbur that by helping him to live perhaps she was trying to lift up her own life a little, and I would spare the web.

And then I noticed that I would come upon a spider in the garage, would be about to swat it when I would hear the voice of Debbie Reynolds singing the Sherman Brothers song "Mother Earth and Father Time." And I couldn't bring myself to take a life just because it had four pairs of legs, eight eyes, and a bad reputation.

I am convinced that Charlotte's kinfolk took advantage of Jane and me. I am sure the word spread throughout the spider world that the Hamners were suckers for spiders.

Each morning the rose garden would be garlanded with new webs. The path to the vegetable garden would be hung with sticky netting that had not been there before I went to bed. An ambitious female spider would show off and establish an anchor to her web high in the elm tree near the back door. From the anchor lines she would branch out, catch the wind to attach another line to the maple tree, then up again until she had a center built, and then going round and round from the center she would form a vast perfectly formed net. With the coming of daylight the net would be laced with moths, gnats, flies, crickets, bees, and grasshoppers.

The whole tribe was bloodthirsty. I found this out as I watched through a magnifying glass as one of them rolled its prey into a small round ball and then proceeded to suck out its juices. Moving on to another net I discovered that this was how they spent their days.

Accidentally walking full faced into a spider web is an awful experience. You brush it away frantically, hoping that the spider is not stuck somewhere in your hair. For the next several minutes phantom tickles break out all over your face. Then for the better part of an hour you pick sticky silk strands from behind your ears or away from your glasses or from around your collar. Later in the day you run your hands through your hair and feel a particle of something. When you finally isolate it, you discover that it's the dried husk of some insect left over from the web.

In spite of all this potential trauma, we felt it was wrong to destroy the webs and there came a time when Jane and I

were ducking under webs, or stepping over them and taking
different paths through the yard to avoid them.

We considered using a chemical spray but we couldn'
bring ourselves to do it. We kept telling ourselves that they
had as much right to the earth as we did, that they were
beneficial because their diet consisted mainly of insects, and
that we had a special relationship with them because I had
written the *Charlotte's Web* screenplay.

There was one spider in particular. If I disturbed his home
he would scamper to the edge of the net and there he would
jump up and down on his tiny banded legs as if scolding me fo
having troubled him. What an arrogant little beast! I frequently
was tempted to remind him who the boss was in my yard.

And then one night I was reading quite late, and
became aware that I was sharing my bed with an uninvited
guest. I threw back the covers and there was a fat or
weaver who scampered deep into the covers and disap
peared. I pulled the bed apart and only when I thought tha
the intruder was gone was I able to get back to my book.

I continued reading and then over the top edge of th
book appeared a pair of spindly legs. A row of eyes fol
lowed. Rigid with apprehension I watched while the dam
thing crawled right over the edge and down the inner spin
of the book. When I shook the book he jumped up and
down indignantly.

Reason, and freedom from any obligation to my youn
fans or to E. B. White finally triumphed. I freed myself o
Charlotte's Web! I slammed the pages of the book together.

It felt good!

12. House on Nude Beach Invaded by Rodent!

Talmadge the mouse came into our lives in the summer of 1969. I wrote two movies that year: *Where the Lilies Bloom* and *Charlotte's Web*. By Hollywood's standards I received minimal fees, but to a child of the Depression the money seemed phenomenal. We decided to buy a beach house. When looking for a place at the beach many people here look to Malibu, but the water there is murky, the real estate prices are outrageous, and the way of life is self-conscious, closeted and isolated from the real world.

We opted for Laguna Beach, a democratic, quaint, and extremely beautiful village that curves around the shoreline as it reaches up from San Clemente toward Newport Beach. Jane had lived there as a child, and in our visits to the scenes of her growing-up, we had fallen in love with the place. Scott and Caroline shared our enthusiasm and joined in searching for a beach house. We tramped through one stunning home after another, none of which we could afford, even with my newfound wealth.

Finding nothing within our price range to buy, we rented a small, comfortable house on Tortuva Cove, a small private beach in South Laguna.

Tortuva Cove is a three-quarter-mile stretch of sand and surf. Most of the homes are located on a high bluff. Access to the beach is attained by long stairways that curve back upon themselves several times in their descent from the bluffs down to the sand. Passage to the area along the beach itself is blocked at either end by massive rock formations. Crossing them to reach the adjacent beaches is nearly impossible at high tide and even at low tide somewhat perilous.

The southernmost area of the beach is populated by free thinkers and nudists. The northernmost end is dominated by a condominium complex where the more well-to-do and more conservative folks have staked their claim. The two factions provide endless drama. The strait-laced condo-folk constantly are calling the police to report the nudists. In retaliation, the nudists stage raucous, lascivious, and fascinating parties at night in enemy territory, directly in front of the condos. Jane and Scott and Caroline and I found ourselves in the middle, polarized, neither to the north nor the south end of the beach. We were comfortably in between.

On a clear day you could, as the saying goes, see Catalina. We were enchanted with the cove, wanted to live there for the rest of our lives, and were delighted when we learned of a home for sale only a few doors away.

We were committed from the moment we walked into the house. It had been built with some imagination. From outside it had the appearance of a small barn and it was located on a bluff with a stunning view. From every room we looked down into the turquoise cove where the blue-green water washed ashore in an endless white surf. From the broad picture windows we witnessed a parade of sailboats, fishing boats, pelicans, surfers, nudists, joggers, gulls, swimmers, and conservative strollers carrying, so help me, parasols.

Twice a year we observed the most magical passage of all: the migration of the whales. They were gray whales, still not an uncommon sight along the West Coast. In late December and January they would pass before us on their way to Scammons Lagoon in Mexico where they would journey to deliver their young. At the Easter season we would see them making their way northward, this time with their offspring swimming beside them.

The passing of the whales was a spectacle that always created excitement along the beach. A geyser of water would signal their presence, and then a cry would go up from the south end of the cove:

"Whales offshore!"

And the cry would spread northward until all of us would converge on our decks to watch whatever the behemoths would show of themselves. Sometimes the display consisted only of a flume of white water spouting into the air like a fountain. Often, if we were lucky, we could catch sight of something the size of a freight train, leaping into the air making a majestic arc, suspended like some enormous

ballet dancer in the air. We could discern small eyes, barna-
cles on its undersides, and the display would end with a slap
of its monstrous tail as it sank back into the sea and out of
our vision. As brief as these encounters were, we felt we had
shared, if even for a moment, communion with some
ancient and ineffably mysterious form of life.

Smaller, but no less interesting creatures lived in close
proximity. There was a strikingly marked black and white
skunk who lived under the stairs leading down to the house.
Periodically he would lean out mischievously and spray one
of our dogs. We would have to spend hours giving the dogs
repeated baths in tomato juice. There were hundreds of
garter snakes, which would put an abrupt end to my gardening when I recognized that the thing I was pulling from
around the root of the oleander was not a tendril of crab-
grass but something reptilian. There was a ground squirrel
that made so many burrows underneath our embankment
that we worried for a while that our entire house might tum-
ble into the sea.

But most of all there was Talmadge.

Sometimes on Friday nights, if we were able to get away
from Los Angeles in time to escape the worst of the freeway
traffic, we would head for the beach house. After a dinner of
scallops and white wine at the small restaurant on the Coast
Highway, we would unpack, and after the children were
asleep we would sit quietly and rest our minds and bodies
from the toll the stressful week had taken.

From our chairs in the living room we could observe the

itchen and it was there one night that we first observed
Talmadge brazenly searching for food. He emerged from the
eneral area behind the refrigerator and then skittered across
ne floor in a search that was frantic, comical, and desperate.

"There's a mouse in the kitchen," said Jane.

"I'll set a trap in the morning," I said.

"Why are you so bloodthirsty?" she asked. "It's only a
nouse."

"They multiply," I answered.

"Good," said Jane. "It might be nice to have a family of
nem around. They'll keep the crumbs off the floor."

"Suppose I go out into the kitchen for a beer one night in
ne dark and step on one?" I asked.

"You drink more beer than is good for you," said Jane.

"I drink it for digestive reasons," I countered.

"An antacid would do the same thing and be much better
or you," she said.

"It wouldn't take the place of the beer," I said. "And it
elps me get to sleep when I go to bed."

"Sometimes by the time you go to bed, you're a little
onfused," she observed.

Sometimes by the time I went to bed, I was a little plas-
red, but I wasn't about to admit that, and Jane was con-
derate enough not to mention it.

By this time, Talmadge was rushing about in the kitchen
a desperate and fruitless search for food.

"That mouse is hungry," said Jane, who could never
sist feeding any hungry creature. "I'm going to feed it." She

proceeded to place on a paper plate five cashew nuts, a slab of peanut butter (extra-crunchy), two leftover scallops which we had brought home in a doggie bag to feed to the seagulls, a leaf of lettuce, and some dog vitamins.

"Poor thing looks starved to death," she said when she returned to her chair. "Skinny as a rail." Talmadge had disappeared when Jane entered the kitchen, but he came out seconds later and began sampling the smorgasbord.

There was a kind of madness in his eyes that could only be relieved by gifts of food. We tried refusing him seconds. We would turn away when he appeared at the railing of the kitchen where he would sit upright on his haunches and look at us imploringly.

"That mouse needs to go on a diet," I said.

"I'll just give him a lettuce leaf," said Jane.

Talmadge spurned the lettuce leaf. He was mad for fat and calories.

We ignored him for the remainder of the evening, but whenever our gaze would go to the railing of the kitchen, we would see him there, sitting on his haunches like a begging dog and looking at us accusingly.

Talmadge grew to trust us. On the following weekends, as soon as we walked in the door, he appeared at the corner of the refrigerator and looked up as if to say, "What's for dinner?"

"I think you've made a friend," I said to Jane.

"Then I'll just have to stop being his friend," she said. "Wild things can't forage for themselves if they become too dependent on humans."

"We could feed him only on the weekend," I offered, because secretly I had begun to enjoy Talmadge's company and the constancy with which he appeared and greeted us each time we visited the beach house.

"If he's only fed on weekends, what's he going to do for food during the week?" asked Jane sensibly. I had no reply to that.

We refused to feed Talmadge from then on. We would turn away when he appeared at the railing of the kitchen.

"Maybe a peanut?" I suggested when I could stand his imploring look no longer.

"It's not right," said Jane. "He's becoming too dependent on us."

We did not feed the mouse again. We did leave water in the dog's dish every Monday morning when we left the beach to go back to Studio City.

One weekend we overlooked a bowl of peanuts on the coffee table when we left. On our next visit, his droppings and the empty bowl assured us that Talmadge had not gone hungry during our absence.

The next weekend Talmadge did not greet us, but he betrayed his presence during the night when we heard a small crash from the kitchen. When we went to investigate, we discovered that he had found a bag of walnuts we had left on top of the refrigerator. He had systematically removed most of them and hidden them in some secret place.

"They're not good for him," said Jane. "They're just laden with cholesterol."

We placed what remained of the walnuts in the refrigerator and went back to bed.

Next Talmadge began raiding the dogs' food. We still had the cocker spaniels, Clemmentine and Chloe, in those days, but they had grown old, given to tics, nervousness, and hallucinations. It only took the approach of Talmadge at the edge of their food dishes to send them howling in terror into the bedroom where they would hide until we would coax them out again. By that time Talmadge would have consumed as much of their food as he required and would have turned in for the night. We suspected he lived somewhere behind the refrigerator but it was not until sometime later that we could come to know that we had guessed correctly.

We became more and more careful about leaving food of any kind available when we left the house. As careful as we were, we inadvertently forgot and left a box of dog biscuits sitting on the counter. When we came back on Friday night the box of dog biscuits had been overturned and the box was empty.

We caught sight of Talmadge just one more time. He had grown into an obese gray blob. He no longer skittered with awkward grace along the floor. He waddled like Templeton the Rat in *Charlotte's Web*. Even his tail had lost its erect, rudder-like carriage. It drooped behind him listlessly. He looked at us once, but it was the look of a friend who has been offended and doesn't want to be friends any longer. There was even a hint, or so we thought, of malevolence in his quick last glance in our direction.

When we entered the house the following Friday night, we were met by the stench of something dead. We opened every window in the house, but still the odor persisted.

We decided that the odor was coming from somewhere in the kitchen and spent considerable time moving the refrigerator.

There behind it, stuck in the hole he had gnawed in order to gain entry, was Talmadge. His enormous body was wedged firmly in the hole and he had been able to go neither forward nor backward, and there, trapped by his greed, he had died.

I found a work glove, picked up the remains and threw them into the ice plant far below. As I returned to the house, I began composing words with which to console Jane, who does not take comfort from the death of any living thing.

"I'm sure he died happy," I began. "At least he was never hungry."

"I just hope he didn't leave any relatives behind," said Jane.

Several weeks later when another mouse made an appearance in our kitchen, without proclamation I set a trap for it. If Jane ever noticed it, she made no comment.

13. Dog Gives Life for Love!

Gus was illegal. We had him with us for the shortest period we ever owned any dog, but somehow his memory fades the least of all.

What made Gus illegal was that we had our quota of dogs when he came to us. Actually, we were over our quota, for there were five dogs calling our house home when the city of Los Angeles permitted only four dogs per residence. Unless of course the family took out a license and had the home declared a kennel. And that was considered at one point.

One of our neighbors at the time was the actress Nancy Kulp. She played the secretary to the banker on *The Beverly Hillbillies*. On screen, Miss Kulp portrayed a strident, overly precise, and wonderfully amusing secretary. In real life, Nancy was a delightful, warm, witty, socially aware and concerned human being. After she retired from acting she ran for public office in her native Pennsylvania. Except for her work on film, she is no longer with us, but the work lives on celluloid as does a fond memory.

Nancy had become a friend of our children's. She allowed them, and our entire neighborhood gang, to make a shortcut through her yard on their way to and from the Carpenter Avenue School, which saved them considerable time and distance.

Prior to this, the kids had made a shortcut through Robert Bolling's yard. Robert, a gentleman in his eighties, had recently taken a new wife. The detour became necessary when Robert requested that the children no longer come through his yard because he informed us that he and Jessica were fond of making love out-of-doors and he did not want the children to come across any surprises.

One night at dinner, Caroline announced, "Nancy's got about a hundred puppies."

"Sixteen," said Scott.

"Don't correct me," rejoined Caroline, who was sensitive to being corrected and had a mind of her own.

"Sixteen," said Scott, who did not give up easily.

"Hundred," said Caroline, who did not give up easily either.

"What's she going to do with all of them?" asked Jane.

"When they're eight weeks old, she's going to give them away," replied Caroline. "How many do you want, Mom?"

Jane considered the question seriously. We had seen the mother dog. She was a cockapoo of a vague apricot color and a face that was appealing, intelligent, and irresistible.

"I'll take the whole litter," said Jane.

"Now hold on!" I said.

"Just kidding," said Jane.

"Thank God!" I said. "Any more dogs around here are just out of the question."

"The ones that Nancy can't find homes for will have to go to the pound," said Scott with a meaningful look to his mother.

"They die horribly there," said Caroline. "They inject oxygen in their veins and when it reaches their hearts they explode all over the place."

"Boom!" said Scott.

"Kerplow!" said Caroline.

Jane showed what I took to be a sign of sanity. I recognized it later as simply a delaying action.

"We are already over the legal limit with dogs. We simply cannot take in another one." And she left the table.

Secret looks passed between Scott and Caroline. If I had been a truly perceptive parent, I would have recognized then that mischief was afoot.

There was at that time, across from our house, a big, open, sunny hillside, which we called "the field." It was where I flew my kites when the wind was right, and the place where I intended someday to release a covey of bob-white quail.

The gang of children on the street had built a clubhouse in the field. It was only after they were grown that they told me that the clubhouse was used for smoking marijuana, experimenting with sex, and detailed planning to overthrow all of adult society.

Jane and I gradually became aware that someone or something had taken up residence in the field. Our children would linger there until the last minute before dinner and would return there every evening until darkness fell or until we called them home. Sly looks would be exchanged among our children and their friends. Table scraps wrapped in paper napkins would mysteriously disappear at the end of meals.

There were no coyotes in "the field" in those days. At least they were not as numerous then as they are now. On occasions, we would allow the children to sleep in their clubhouse overnight. Increasingly, one or more of the children would request permission to sleep over in the clubhouse.

Being a freelance writer, my hours were flexible. I would have meetings at odd hours during the day, and occasionally I would drop by the house for lunch with Jane.

One day I went home for lunch. Jane was out. There was a stillness in the neighborhood. The children, whose playful shouts and shrieks would later shatter all peace in the neighborhood, were at school. The air was still and quiet.

I made my lunch and took the sandwich on a paper plate down by the pool to eat it. As I sat there, I heard a sound. It was a lonesome sound, the plea of a homeless or motherless animal, a plaintive cry for companionship. It came from the direction of the children's clubhouse in the field.

I walked over to the field and, as I approached the clubhouse, I could hear the sound more clearly. As if it sensed my nearness, whatever was making the sound increased its volume and intensity.

I pushed open the door to the clubhouse. There in the corner the children had made a dog bed. In it, looking up, was a round ball of curly brown fluff, one ear perked inquisitively. It was the most appealing puppy I had ever seen.

I hardened my heart and stayed there until the children came home from school. They were somewhat surprised to find me in the clubhouse, but they listened attentively while I explained that if their mother were to see the puppy, there would be no way in the world she could resist him. I explained that we were already over our legal quota and that if she were to take in another dog there was a good possibility she might cause us all to go to jail.

I pleaded with them to find a home for the puppy before Jane came home, and then I went back to my office to work on *The Twilight Zone* episode I was writing.

That evening when I arrived home, there was no dinner in preparation, no family to greet me at the door. My family and all the kids in the neighborhood were down on the floor of the kitchen. They were taking turns petting the "new" puppy we had acquired. They had named him Gus.

"Where did that come from?" I asked.

"He was wandering around in the road just as I came home from the market," said Jane. "The poor little thing could have been run over!"

"You were set up!" I tried to explain. "These treacherous children turned him loose just as you were turning the curve."

"Isn't he adorable?" she responded.

"Adorable and illegal!" I exploded. "Jane, we can't keep this animal!"

"Oh," she said. "I know that. We're just going to take him in for the night. Give him a little food and water. First thing in the morning, we'll take him to the Pound."

She gave me a look of such innocence that I had to take her word for the truth.

On our way to the Pound the next morning, Jane held Gus, and I drove.

"They keep them at least fourteen days before they put them to sleep," Jane observed.

"He's sure to find a good home," I assured her.

"Sometimes they don't even try to find homes for them," she said. "They sell them to cosmetics companies who use them for experimental purposes."

"They wouldn't do that with a nice little dog like him," I said.

"I'm sure they wouldn't," she said. "Him, they'd probably turn over to one of the medical schools where they dissect them. First they test them to see how long they can go without sleep or food or water. Sometimes they go mad before the interns can finish their experiments."

I made a U-turn in the middle of Ventura Boulevard and took Jane and our new, illegal dog back to Avocado Drive.

Gus had only one problem. He was horny twenty-four

hours a day. If a lady dog three miles away went into heat, Gus knew it, and he would go in search of her. Whenever he was missing, we only had to call around until we found out what female was in heat to know where to look for him.

One night I arrived home from work to find Jane looking somewhat concerned. When I asked why, she said, "It's rather indelicate. Just look at Gus."

I looked at Gus and noticed nothing unusual.

"What about Gus?" I asked.

"He has an erection," she said.

"Gus always has an erection," I said.

"But he's had this one for two days. He's walking funny and seems to be in pain," said Jane.

"It's nothing to worry about," I said. "Nature takes care of itself."

But that was not the case. The following morning, Gus was in great discomfort, and the erection was still there.

"Can I tell the doctor what the problem is?" asked the nurse in Dr. Garner's office when I called.

"I'd rather tell him myself," I said.

"He can't come to the phone right now, but I can repeat your message to him and perhaps he can help you."

"It's Gus," I said.

"I hope he's all right," said the nurse. "He's such a little doll."

"He has an erection," I said.

"Sounds like him," she said.

"It won't go away," I said.

"Hold on," she said, and I could hear her talking to Dr. Garner at the other end of the phone.

"The doctor says 'Put ice on it'," said the nurse. She was trying to remain professional, but her voice broke and she began to giggle.

Gus at first looked at us in an offended way when we began massaging his groin with ice, but gradually when the burden of his erection began to ease, his whole body seemed to relax, and he looked to us in what I assumed to be gratitude.

His passion knew no limits. No female dog was too large or too small to engage his desire. Often his amorous advances were comical, and sometimes dangerous, especially if he were in competition with a larger male. And that we think led to his undoing.

Her name was Sweet Pea, and if there is any such thing as an ugly dog, Sweet Pea was one. She had an underslung jaw, matted gunmetal hair, and crazy eyes. She was short. She did not walk; she waddled. Even so, every male dog in the neighborhood was crazy about her.

She could have had her choice of any dog in the neighborhood, but she loved Gus. Even when she was not in heat, she would come calling for him every morning. She would sit outside our gate and wait until I walked the dogs. As soon as we came out of the gate, she would fall in companionably beside Gus and go on our walk with us.

Her owners were irresponsible and allowed her total freedom. That was well and good for Sweet Pea, but it caused those of us in the neighborhood who owned male dogs a great deal of concern.

Gus somehow got out of the yard, and he was gone overnight. We called him and we looked everywhere. We checked with the Animal Regulation people, but none of them had any record of an animal answering Gus's description.

We found him around noon the following day. He had crawled into some underbrush down below the clubhouse. Sweet Pea, who was still in heat, had kept vigil beside his body. He was not yet dead, but he had been badly mauled by some other, larger dog, and was little more than a pathetic misshapen lump of fur.

We took him to Dr. Garner, who did not offer much hope. Nevertheless, he did what he could. Jane stayed there at the hospital for two days and kept vigil, but Gus never regained consciousness.

I sometimes ask myself what rewards there might have been to Gus's short life, and I console myself with the fact that he knew high passion, that he was adored by all who knew him, and that even though it led to his death, he spent most of his life questing for love and that, more often than not, he found it.

14. Hero Flies with Flock of Birds! Labrador Retriever Unreliable Witness!

I once came into unexpectedly close contact with a flock of birds. It was the nearest I have ever come to experiencing what it might be like to be other than human. For one brief, ecstatic, mystical moment I shed every human attribute and became as one with a swirling, lilting, soaring mass of winged creatures.

Many varieties of wild birds either live with us or visit seasonally on Avocado Drive. Jane invites them by providing facilities for feeding and bathing. They are attracted, too, by the plantings that provide them food and nesting sites.

There is a family of red-tailed hawks that make their home in a canyon a half mile down the road. They have called upon us, at least to my knowledge the male has. I came upon him unexpected, as I made my morning inspection of the backyard. He was perched on top of an aviary that housed our family of white doves. He gave me an insolent, inquiring look with his savage eyes while I gazed at him in admiration and astonishment.

In what could have been a stupid impulse, I decided to try to make contact. I had seen falconers induce their falcons to come to them by raising their arms as a perch and by whistling.

I whistled an approximation of the sound I remembered the falconer made, and then I raised my arm. When I did, the hawk decided to move, not to me, but insolently into the air with a quick, commanding flap of his iridescent wings. He rose through the branches of the wild walnut tree and then he was gone. God knows what damage he might have done to my arm had he accepted my invitation to perch on it. I imagine I would still bear the scars, but what I yearned for was still not as frivolous as it may have seemed. I wanted contact with that wild and beautiful thing. I wanted to feel the beat of its heart, to know it, to surmount the lack of communication that was between the hawk and me. I passionately wanted to fly with him.

We think the hawk paid us another visit because one morning we found three of the doves dead in the aviary. We surmised that the hawk was the murderer. The damage was done in such a way that the flesh and the feathers had been torn from their bodies by a predator reaching through the wire walls of the cage.

One group of birds that have accepted Jane's hospitality is a colony of blue jays. They are bold birds, or maybe they are simply gullible, almost too trusting of humans. For a while there was one so tame that we simply had to open the kitchen door and he would fly in and perch on the back of a rocking chair. He would appraise the situation and then fly over to the counter where Jane stored peanuts, help himself to one, and then fly back out of doors again. Within two or three minutes he would repeat the performance and would continue to repeat it as long as the door was left open.

Contact with the particular blue jay was easy. I had only to hold a peanut in the palm of my hand and he would appear on the branch of a tree, hop from it with a determined dive, perch on one of my fingers long enough to gain hold of the peanut, and tilt his head as he looked me over. Then he would fly off to hide it before he returned for more.

The blue jay gave me nothing of what I yearned for, no sense of flight, no sense of what it was to be a bird. There was only the quick pinch of his toes around my finger, the sensation of holding some live, incredibly weightless, living thing and then it was gone.

The most frequent and numerous guests at Jane's feeder are families of California mourning doves. Some mornings twenty or thirty of them are gathered for breakfast at the feeder. They are plump and dun-colored. They feed nervously, and often there are exhibitions of hostility as they fly at one another or peck some undesirable member of the flock in a show of the pecking order—a ritual that all fowl seem to accept as necessary.

The doves are swift of flight and do not always observe caution. Occasionally one of them will not pay attention to where it is going and will fly into the window, leaving the powdery imprint of its breast on the glass.

We have learned to look for such accident victims in the shrubbery. If it is not dead, the injured bird will often die of heart failure when it is picked up by a human hand. There have been other times when we have been able to keep a stunned, and not too badly injured, dove alive long enough for it to recover from its shock and fly to freedom.

As satisfying as it may be to nurse a stunned dove back to flight, it still never satisfied my yearning to know flight, to know what it is like to *be* a bird.

And yet, astonishingly and in the most amazing way, it happened. I was given a moment that I suspect few of us have experienced, one certainly that I will never forget.

Yarrow, the white Labrador Scott had given us, and I had walked to the end of Avocado Drive and back again. He had not felt a call to nature, so I extended our walk to the dead end of the street where there is an elm tree and a commanding view of the San Fernando Valley. Yarrow paced about moodily, searching for a spot that was acceptable to him.

I looked across the violet lights of the valley, clear as water in the fresh morning air, and then to the sharply etched silhouette of the San Gabriel Mountains, which rise on the opposite side of the valley.

To the east a sizable black cloud appeared. It did not follow the moving pattern of any cloud I had ever seen, but moved with speed and with a constantly changing shape, one minute a perfect oval, the next a long thin line that would change abruptly to a circle. As it came closer I realized that it was not a cloud, but an enormous mass of flying birds. I did not recognize what kind of birds they were. Perhaps they were some migrating species on their way to or from Mexico, for we are on the flyway of a good many migrating birds.

As I watched, they came closer, and then almost before I knew what was happening, the first wave of them swerved down and in front of me. I was surrounded by a dense mass of tiny bodies that were hurling through space. I could hear the private churring of their voices, the slap of their wings against their bodies, the whistle of the wind as they scissored through the opposing air. Small darting eyes looked into mine, their feet extended behind them were folded so as not to impede the drag of the wind. I was in exultation in their presence, their sound, their being, by their mass and by their movement, I became one of them, knew the tiny beating of their hearts, felt the toughness of their wing muscles, felt the ecstasy of being borne upon the air on wings, lifted heavenward—the bonds of Earth broken, knew finally the experience of flight, for they had shared it with me.

They were gone as suddenly as they had arrived. I cannot account for it. Perhaps I was in the path of their flight pattern. Perhaps they were momentarily off their course.

When they were gone, I looked down to Yarrow and said, "My God, Yarrow! We flew!"

And he looked up to me with his elegant, trusting eyes as if to say, "If you say so."

15. *Willie Is Not What He Seems to Be!*

We were told that the male rat made the better pet. The male, so we were told, tends to have a more even disposition. It is less prone to moods and indisposition than the female. It could with patience and the proper training become an affectionate and responsive companion.

We were doing this research because Caroline had requested that Santa Claus bring her a rat for Christmas. Jane and I resisted the idea and attempted to talk our daughter out of it. She seemed much more the type for old-fashioned dolls, fairy-tale books and "tea sets." But at the time she had a friend who had an inoffensive white rat that would ride about on the friend's shoulders, allow itself to be cuddled and displayed. It even seemed to enjoy being scratched and petted. Caroline could not be talked out of her yearning, and so we went shopping.

At the pet shop, we bought—and were assured that we had paid for—one male white rat. The clerk assured us that the rat had been conditioned to people, and to make his point he insisted I reach into the cage, take out the rat and pet it. This took great effort on my part. Back in the Blue Ridge Mountains where I come from, rats are a nuisance and a menace. Whenever evidence was found that we had an infestation of rats, we would address the problem with traps and poison.

I was constantly having to remind myself we had come a long way from the Blue Ridge Mountains of Virginia. The whole world had changed since my growing-up years. There is even something, unheard of in my childhood, called animal "rights." Certainly rats are included.

There is a rat in California, which, if not a native, should surely qualify. We know it as the tree rat or the Australian ivy rat, for that would seem to be its most comfortable habitat. You catch sight of them occasionally peering cautiously around the edge of an ivy plant, their eyes filled more with curiosity than with fear. Their tails are held at the ready as spare balancing tools in case of sudden flight. In times of their severest infestation, we resort to poison. The poison's effect is to dehydrate the body so thoroughly that all that remains is a distressingly spare hank of hair. Sometimes the four feet are folded inwardly and even more rarely there is the remainder of a head but if one is lucky there are no eyes remaining to communicate what must have been an agonized death.

We find our tree rats appealing. Their ears tend to be long, their eyes inquisitive, and their coats a soft blue-gray not unlike the coat of a chinchilla. We kill them, but regretfully.

Perhaps when it came time to bring a rat into the house, it was the appeal of the natives that made it easier for us to accept the idea of a rodent as a pet. At any rate, we gave in and bought the fellow a respectable cage and laid in provisions for him.

On Christmas morning, Caroline spotted the rat and chose him for her favorite present that year. I think the gift was a genuine surprise to her because she knew we had reservations.

She named him Willie, and because Caroline is a sensitive and gentle person, Willie seemed to know that he could trust her, and almost immediately she had tamed him.

A few days after Christmas, Willie began to show signs of restiveness. He would pace around the cage at night when we felt he should be sleeping. He would rush about frantically, turning over his food dish and upsetting his watering dish. We made a nest of excelsior for him. He charged at the nest, destroyed it, and then rebuilt it again more to his liking.

I decided that perhaps his uneasiness might be relieved if I petted him. I reached into his cage and picked him up gently, and that was when Willie gave me a nip on the finger—a sharp bite that hurt like hell. I warned Caroline that Willie was not to be trusted. I suggested that perhaps we should work together with him a bit more until we were sure that he was more trustworthy. But even though we gave Willie every consideration, he continued his strange behavior. He went without sleep and paced in his cage incessantly.

There were other interests to occupy us for the remainder of the Christmas season, and it was in the back of my mind that once the pet shop opened, Caroline and I might take Willie down there and trade him in. Perhaps a more trustworthy pet might be selected. I had not suggested this to Caroline for, in spite of his idiosyncratic behavior, she had become fond of Willie, and I doubted that she would agree to trading him in.

On the first day of the new year, Jane called me at the office. She was laughing, but there was another ingredient in her voice. Hysteria, maybe?

"It's Willie," she said.

"What about Willie?" I asked.

"I'm looking in the cage right this minute," said Jane, "and so far he's had six—no, make that seven, there's another one on the way at this very minute—babies!"

There were ten in the litter. There were two, which might have been runts, that simply never really came to life. Two others disappeared. There was some conjecture that Willie ate them, but we've never been sure of that, so we decided to believe that they simply vanished.

Caroline decided that Willie was an unsuitable name for her rat and rechristened her Willamina. Willamina's disposition changed totally, and she became as tame and as engaging a pet as we've ever had.

Disposing of a litter of rats can put a strain on relationships. Friends with children the same ages as ours avoided us until they were sure we would not attempt to foist off our extra baby rats on them. Those friends who did take pity on us and accepted one of our excess rodents as a favor seldom called again. The lady in the pet shop where we had originally purchased Willie/Willamina agreed to accept a few of the overflow, but finally we ended up with Willamina and three of her offspring as permanent members of the zoo.

One of them, a male, escaped and was never seen again, although there exists some evidence that he lived a merry and morally irresponsible existence in his free state.

Willamina and her two daughters lived for several years. They grew obese and as lazy as sloths. Sometimes Caroline and her friends would take them from their cages, but because of their weight problems, Willamina and her daughters were not much fun. Their only real interest in life was food. The only time they showed any animation was when we filled their food dishes. Once, we decided they should diet and began cutting back on the amounts we fed them, but they developed anxieties and we returned to feeding them copious amounts of food and they returned to their obesity.

That summer there came a heat spell of such intensity and longevity that we all nearly perished. Day after heat-laden day would come. The air was like liquid fire and we moved through it as though through some viscous substance. We took pains to see that every member of the zoo had fresh water and in ample amounts. We also checked on them at different times during the day. In an attempt to keep cool, each rat stretched itself across the bottom of its cage, spreadeagle fashion. Even their fat pink tails were collapsed.

We became suspicious when they remained in that position even after sundown when the temperatures began to diminish and we received some relief from the merciless sunlight.

But the rats remained prostrate. Worried that she might have been overcome by the heat, we picked up Willamina and examined her. Our suspicions were correct. Willamina and each of her daughters were near death. We stayed up most of the night, wrapping them in damp, cool towels and force-feeding them with water, but by dawn all three of them were dead.

As I mentioned, we never knew exactly what happened to the male that escaped. But we did have some indication of how he fared in the wilds. The following spring when our annual wave of tree rats began their invasion, there was something new in their appearance. Instead of their being solid blue-gray, they were multicolored and more than one of them wore a dappled coat. And even now, all these many years later, it is not unusual for us to spot a descendant of Willamina's still sporting a spot or two of her beautiful white fur.

16. Virginia Relative Arrives
with Mysterious Object in Pillowcase!

———— ◆ ————

While waiting for my nephew Nay Hankins by the baggage counter at LAX, I reflected on how long it had been since I had last seen him. Some six years had passed since I had visited his family in Roanoke, Virginia. I remembered a long, lanky, handsome kid, already reaching for height and grace.

Nay is the son of my sister Audrey. She is the mother of a sprawling gang of big-shouldered, narrow-hipped, disarmingly frank and attractive boys and one daughter, the petite and beautiful Wendy.

Audrey raised the children well. Among other things she did right was to buy a house that bordered on a national forest. With the forest as a backyard, the kids grew to know and love all the green and growing things that lived there. They could identify over a hundred wild herbs and flowers, knew by their tracks what wild animal had passed during the night, knew which were the edible mushrooms and which were poisonous toadstools. They knew how to snare a rabbit, how to cook a 'possum, where the striped bass would school in Smith Mountain Lake, and what bait to use to lure them to the hook. If the Hankins boys had one consuming passion, it was snakes.

I recalled that the last time I had visited the farm outside of Roanoke, on the back porch there had been a large fish tank that contained a miniature landscape. A decaying log ran the length of the tank. There was a small pond, some autumn leaves, some stones arranged as carefully as in a Zen garden. Unaccountably, a small mouse seemed the only occupant of the terrarium.

"That's a nice home you've made for your mouse," I observed to Nay.

"Better not look if you're squeamish," replied Nay.

As squeamish as I am, I looked.

And then I discerned something so artfully camouflaged that I had not seen it before: a beautifully patterned, rigid, coiled diamond-back rattlesnake. As I watched, its triangular head rose ever so slowly and then shot forward toward the mouse. The force of the blow sent the mouse to the far end of the tank. On its back, with its tiny legs clawing the air, the mouse laid as the snake glided casually in for its meal.

I reflected on this memory while waiting for Nay, for in addition to their love of the wilderness, the Hankins boys had a fine sense of drama, and it was not without reason that I suspected Nay's arrival would provide some excitement.

At the far end of the baggage counter, I spotted Nay. He towered above the other travelers, his disarmingly curious country boy's eyes easing about the terminal, absorbing and appraising his surroundings, only partly oblivious to the admiring looks he received from every female in the room.

He was carrying a pillowcase neatly tied at the top with a length of cord. Inside the pillowcase there appeared to be something the size of a ten-pound sack of sugar. That something appeared to be in slow, constant, undulating movement. Nay and I greeted each other and waited for his luggage to appear on the gondola.

The last time we had seen him had been on his return from Alaska, where he had lived in a tepee and earned his meals by reciting Robert Service poems in bars.

"Your letter didn't say what you've been doing out west this time," I said.

"Counselor at a boys' camp in Nevada," replied Nay. "Up in the mountains. You got a shower at your house?"

I assured him that we did.

"Good," he said. "I been taking baths in creeks."

"What's in the pillowcase, Nay?" I asked.

"Tell you when we get home," he replied.

You don't push Audrey's boys. They tell what's in the bag when they're ready.

Once we had collected his duffel bag and carried it to the car, Nay sat in the passenger seat and placed the undulating pillowcase on the floor.

"How was Nevada?" I asked.

"Got chased ten miles by a bear," he replied.

"What would a bear want with you?" I asked, knowing I had been prompted.

"Wasn't me he was after," Nay answered. "He smelled that extra-large Hershey Bar with almonds I had in the pocket of my jacket."

"I judge the bear didn't catch you," I said.

"Oh, he caught me all right," said Nay. He fell silent and I let it ride for almost a mile before I bit.

"He didn't kill you, did he?" I asked.

"No, sir," said Nay, "but he made me share that extra-large Hershey Bar with almonds. By the time he'd finished his half, I was long gone for California."

I had no cause to doubt the story until about seven years later, when under somewhat the same circumstances I picked up Nay's younger brother, Joe, at the airport. Joe reported the same adventure almost word for word. My father had the same facility for tall tales, and it is said in our family that as long as Audrey's boys are alive, my father will never die.

Jane, Scott, and Caroline were waiting when Nay and I arrived home.

"I've worn these clothes for three months and been bathing in creeks and chased by a bear," were Nay's opening lines to my children. He won their admiration immediately. We assembled in the living room where Nay still carried the pillowcase. Not without some sense of drama, Nay pretended to ignore it. It had not stopped writhing since I had first laid eyes on it, and I feared what it might contain.

"What's in the pillowcase, Nay?" demanded Caroline.

"You really want to know?" asked Nay.

"Sure," said Caroline, with a shiver of anticipation.

Nay looked to me. A small teasing smile lurked at the corner of his mouth. "You got a snakebite kit in the house? One of them little tubes with a razor blade and a shot of antivenom serum?"

"There's one in the medicine cabinet," I said.

"Then I reckon it's safe," Nay said. He leaned over and released the cord that secured the mouth of the pillowcase. After a moment, movement started in the rear of the bag and progressed toward the opening. Shortly the snout appeared and then the head of a snake. A divided tongue darted in and out, feeling the air, getting a sense of the surroundings. It stopped for a moment and gazed around before it continued its exit. Three feet of snake had emerged by this time, but there was more to follow. It was predominantly brown in a beautiful patterned design that was supplemented by shades of black and russet. On the whole it looked as if it might have been designed by a talented Navaho artist. The snake seemed not the slightest bit nervous, which could not be said for the other occupants of the room.

"Has it got a name?" asked Scott.

"Snake," said Nay.

"Is it from Virginia?" asked Caroline.

"No, ma'am," said Nay. "Come from Nevada. Just outside of camp, right in the middle of the road. The bus driver was about to run over him. I hollered at him just in time. Driver stopped long enough for me to catch him and get back in the bus."

"Dad and I do that with turtles," said Scott.

"I'm glad to hear it," said Nay. "Everything's going to be extinct pretty soon but the automobile if somebody doesn't take that kind of action."

The snake was fully emerged from the pillowcase by now. It was seven feet long with a peculiar oblong lump midway of its length.

"Looks like it has a tumor," said Jane.

"More probably some rabbit it swallowed a day or two ago," said Nay.

"Where are its rattles?" asked Caroline.

"It's not a rattler," explained Nay. "It's a gopher snake. They're good."

The good snake reconnoitered our living room. It froze in place when Eloise, our peach-colored Lhasa apso, entered the room. Dog and snake gazed at each other for a brief moment. When Snake began to move again, Eloise screamed and retreated to a bedroom and would not come out until dinner time.

Later in the evening, I went out on the balcony overlooking the swimming pool to watch the young people taking a dip. There were playing a game called Simon Says, a ferociously active, competitive game. Swimming in the shallow end of the pool, seemingly not the least interested in what the young people were doing, was the seven-foot-long gopher snake, which only twenty-four hours before had been a totally wild thing slithering through the forest of a Nevada wildlife sanctuary.

Two weekends later we went to our house at Laguna Beach. To transport Snake, we found a cat carrier, a cage of ample proportions that could hold him, but give him the freedom to move about and get sufficient exercise. By this time the lump in Snake's midsection had disappeared, and Nay felt that the time had come for Snake to have a feeding.

"We aren't going to feed him anything alive," stated Jane firmly.

"They don't eat anything dead," said Nay.

"Live rabbits are out," said Jane.

"If you'd like to get rid of that Lhasa apso dog, Snake would probably accommodate you," said Nay. "He's been giving her some right favorable looks."

Jane looked to me with her "Do something!" expression.

I suggested that Snake was not going to starve to death and that we would delay his snack for the time being.

In the afternoon, Jane left the house to go shopping for the cookout we were having that evening on the beach.

"I hope Snake don't lose weight," said Nay gloomily as soon as Jane was out of the house.

I am not proud of it, but I wanted to see the snake feed. So did Scott and Caroline. I told myself it would be an educational experience for the children, but to be honest, I wanted to see it happen.

At the pet shop, the clerk did not seem at all pleased by

our request for "something to feed a snake." But Nay persisted and the clerk led us to a cage containing mice. Nay selected four. Two were pure white. One was gray. The fourth was black and white. By the time we returned to the house, the mice had names. They were Eenie, Meenie, Miney, and Moe-Minsky-Pinsky, named after characters in a novel by my friend Don Sipes.

Nay placed the mice in the cat carrier where Snake regarded them with only the faintest interest. The mice, whether or not they had ever seen a snake before, reacted with extreme nervousness. They huddled together in a corner and occasionally one of them would rise on his hind quarters, and then duck back down and shriek some terrified message to his companions.

"Couldn't we feed Snake something else?" asked Caroline.

"That Moe-Minsky-Pinsky looks like he'd make a good pet," said Scott wistfully.

"I'm never going to eat anything that's been alive," declared Caroline.

"I'm going to become a vegetarian," said Scott.

"It's a fact of life that all of us would be dead if we didn't eat something that's been alive at one time or another," said Nay.

Caroline, who until now had adored her cousin, seemed to be having second thoughts. "I think I'll swim out to the rock," she said, and went to change into her bathing suit.

"I've got some reading to do," said Scott and went to the balcony overlooking the living room and opened a book.

"What now?" I asked Nay.

"Ordinarily I just put food in for him. You were the one who wanted to watch."

I was filled with shame. No matter how civilized I had thought myself to be, no matter how I may have deplored cockfighting, bear baiting, and dog fights, some part of my nature I had suppressed had come to the surface. I wondered what my children thought of me. It was clear from Nay's country boy eyes that he had seen this uncivilized side of me before, understood and accepted it. I found some gardening to do, and as I walked away from the cat carrier, I saw that Nay was draping it with a towel.

I admitted to Jane, just before bedtime, that we had placed the mice in the snake's cage, and hoped that they would be gone before morning.

"Don't tell me about it," she said.

The next morning, when I went down for breakfast, Eenie, Meenie, Miney, and Moe-Minsky-Pinsky were alive and living in quarters Jane had set up for them in a shoe box. The mice huddled in a corner and, upon closer observation, I realized that they had gone completely insane. Eenie would suddenly collapse and lie on his back and churn his feet frantically in the air. Meenie would dash from the corner and race around the shoe box until he dropped from exhaustion. Miney seemed catatonic and gazed out upon the world with dull, unseeing eyes, and Moe-Minsky-Pinsky would for no accountable reason leap straight up into the air, come down to earth and repeat the performance over and over.

Jane looked at me reproachfully.

"They've been driven out of their minds," she said.

"How did you get them out of the cat carrier?" I asked.

"I reached in and picked them out," she said.

"Weren't you afraid of the snake?" I asked.

"I was terrified," she answered.

Nay and Snake left for Virginia the middle of the following week. The last I saw of him at the airport, he had his duffel bag over one shoulder and in the other hand he was carrying the pillowcase.

Back in Virginia, because of his size and the fact that he was of the nonpoisonous variety, Snake was given occasional outings in the yard. After one such outing, Snake disappeared. The entire family searched for him, but when there was no trace of him they supposed he had escaped to the national forest that adjoined their backyard.

But one morning, several weeks later, my sister Audrey happened to look out her kitchen window down to the street. It was trash collection day and the sanitation truck was parked in front of the house. The two garbage collectors had withdrawn to the other side of the street and were gesturing wildly to a rapidly collecting crowd of passersby. When a police car arrived and two policemen with drawn revolvers climbed out, Audrey decided she should investigate.

When she came to the front gate, she saw outstretched in front of the garbage cans seven and a half feet of Nevada gopher snake.

To the astonishment of the Sanitation Department, the police with their drawn revolvers, and the passersby, my sister picked him up, draped him over her shoulder and said, "Poor Snake, were these men scaring you?"

Eenie, Meenie, Miney, and Moe-Minsky-Pinsky lived on with us in an elegantly appointed cage that Jane bought for their comfort. They had exercise wheels, cotton nests, a pond for swimming or bathing, and an ample supply of food. But they were never normal mice, and none of them lived for very long.

17. Rescue!

It was that time in southern California when the earth and the air are so parched and baked with heat that it seemed the world might spontaneously combust. Day after day the relentless sun had assaulted us with a dry, searing heat. The sun seemed closer to the parched earth, yellow-hot even as it dawned, and then drew closer and closer overhead as July dragged into August. Even its setting brought no relief. The acrid stench of smog was inescapable.

Night brought a different kind of heat. The air in the house remained still and motionless, heavy with the dry, fragrant desert air. Breathing was difficult. Movement, if one was forced to it, was languid and exhausting.

Still, Yarrow insisted on being taken for his walk.

Yarrow was a Labrador we had inherited when Scott moved into an apartment where pets were not allowed.

Yarrow was a Vermonter by birth, but he adapted quickly to life in California. He was an excellent swimmer and used any excuse to leap into the ocean or the swimming pool.

He was more beautiful than any dog I have ever known. There was nobility in the shape of his head. He had the conformation of a thoroughbred.

He was the noblest of dogs and none of us will ever forget him. I know that he loved us and would have given his life for any one of the family if there had been a need to.

Sometimes it was tempting to forget Yarrow's nightly walk and hope that he would relieve himself in the backyard. But he was a creature of habit and if we did not take him for his walk at the usual time he would find his leash and stand in the doorway holding it in his mouth, all the while wearing an expression as if to say: "I'm going to speak to the ASPCA about you."

In the end one of us would give in and take him out on the street. On hot summer nights, he would plod along, head down, not enjoying the walk, enduring it and sharing the laborious chore before he felt he had put in sufficient time that we could in good conscience return home.

On such a night we had just passed the avocado orchard when Yarrow suddenly froze. In the light of my flashlight, I could see the hairs on his back literally stand straight up. Some surge of energy, something wild, some instinctive protective urge in our domestic pet came alive, and he lunged toward something in the darkness that Jane and I could not see.

And then they came into view: two coyotes, a male and a female. The male was larger, and probably older because his gray coat was tipped with silver. He had only three legs, but the handicap did not greatly hinder his running ability.

Side by side with him ran his mate. She was somewhat smaller, her face more tapered. There was a delicacy about her that was graceful and lovely.

Distracted by trying to control a ninety-pound Labrador outraged that alien creatures had invaded his territory, I struggled with Yarrow. Even with my hands full, I saw the coyotes clearly, felt their nearness enough to know the thirst and hunger that had driven them so close to their enemies.

They disappeared into the darkness almost as quickly as they had come. Jane and I looked to each other with awe that we had been in such close proximity to something so wild and beautiful.

"Poor things," said Jane. "They must be crazed with thirst."

"We'll have to do something about that," I replied.

Yarrow relieved himself soon after that, looking around nervously as he hunched over his business in the hot, dry, furnace-like darkness. And then we returned home.

I remembered a galvanized tin tub in the bath house. We had bought it some years ago to hold some koi eggs that our carp had laid and had immediately begun to eat. There was something especially repellent about seeing the carp consume their own eggs, something akin to witnessing cannibalism. In addition, we had some hopes of raising fish from those eggs. We transferred as many of the eggs as we could retrieve from the pond to the tub. Incredibly, we did actually manage to raise to maturity, out of those millions of randomly laid eggs, one of the fish that hatched. For the moment, the tub was empty and available to provide water for the coyotes.

We placed the tub just to the side of the front gate where, in the dim light from the garage, we could see it from the window of the guest house. Once the tub was filled with water, we went about the evening's business. From time to time, one of us would sneak out to the guest house and check to see if any visitors had come to our watering station.

The following night, just before bedtime, we went together to the guest house. When we looked down into the street we saw the male coyote drinking the water we had set out. As thirsty as he was, he drank cautiously, reminiscent of the way wild birds drink, dropping his head to lap the water then raising it, alert, listening carefully for a moment before going back to slaking his thirst. Finally he looked over his shoulder for a long moment in what might have been a signal, for from the other side of the road, the female appeared. She joined him cautiously and began to drink.

We watched them in wonder and with a feeling of kinship. We were moved that they had accepted our offering and felt a sense of sharing that went beyond species or language.

We had offered comfort and hospitality. They had accepted, and we felt bonded to them. We were awed and humbled. Only when they turned away and padded off into the darkness did we leave the guest house and go to sleep.

In the days that followed, we kept the tub filled with fresh, cool water. We never saw the pair drinking again, but each morning we could tell that they had visited us because the level of the water would be lower than it had been the night before.

The bond between the coyote family and the Hamners deepened. Jane began leaving small gifts: leftover chicken, a steak bone. Being a proper dietitian, she occasionally also set out a leftover salad.

I teased her about the salads but she maintained with lofty authority that all living things need some greens in their diet. It was true that along with the meat course, the salads were gone each morning.

There was a particularly adventuresome and handsome cat in the neighborhood named Ebony. He was a lean, muscular cat, black with a high sheen to his coat. We would spot him occasionally in our backyard when a flash of powerful black muscle would sweep through the flock of doves feeding at our bird station. Then there would be one less dove and one satisfied cat.

Ebony also performed something of a public service by keeping down the gopher population. He would sit for hours, tense and crouched over the entrance to a gopher den, then pounce at just the right moment, fix the unlucky gopher in his teeth and victoriously carry him away. On two occasions we found dead gophers at the back door and we suspected that they were peace offerings Ebony had left in exchange for the doves he had captured.

Ebony belonged to Mr. Rhyder, our neighbor who was an officer with the Department of Animal Regulations and a cowboy by night. Mr. Rhyder's hours were irregular and—we suspected—so was his feeding of his cat.

We never saw Mr. Rhyder show any affection or concern for Ebony. It was our opinion that the cat was neglected or, at best, the two simply tolerated each other.

But one night Ebony disappeared. We took no special notice of his absence. Often days would pass without our catching sight of him, but evidently Ebony and Mr. Rhyder had some agreement about feeding. They might have even had a closer relationship then we thought for when Mr. Rhyder came to our door he was aggrieved and saddened. He was dressed in his cowboy outfit and wore a turquoise bolo tie.

"I can't find Ebony," he said. "I left out some food for him last night and it's still there."

"Oh, he'll be back," I assured him. "Ebony likes to roam. I've seen him all over these hills."

After I assured Mr. Rhyder that we would let him know the minute Ebony reappeared, he seemed placated and returned to his house.

The following morning Mr. Rhyder appeared at our door again. He was carrying a small shopping bag. Inside was a couple of tufts of black fur—all that was left of Ebony.

"It's your coyotes," said Mr. Rhyder.

"What do you mean?" I asked.

"*Your* coyotes," said Mr. Rhyder. "The ones you feed and water every night. Whole packs of them are out by your garage when I come home late at night."

"We do feed them," Jane explained, "but it's just to keep them from getting into this kind of trouble."

"I want it stopped," said Mr. Rhyder firmly. "Or I'll take action," he yelled over his shoulder as he walked away.

We knew Mr. Rhyder to be a man of his word. He had in the past reported neighbors for allowing their grass to grow too high (he considered it a fire hazard). At the first sign of a stranger walking on the street, Mr. Rhyder would report to the police that there was "suspicious behavior" in the neighborhood. Loud children at play, cars with out-of-state license plates, music played past midnight—all were reported to the proper city agencies.

Even so, feeding and watering the coyotes had become a habit with us, almost an obligation, and we continued our nightly chore.

But then we encountered sabotage. Each morning we would find the galvanized watering tub overturned, the precious water spilled onto the street. We suspected Mr. Rhyder, but we had no proof. Driven by the knowledge that hidden in the chaparral were those terribly thirsty creatures, we continued to fill the tub each night. We did not see them often. Our only contact was the watering tub and the sounds of their high, outraged yips when a fire engine would speed down Laurel Canyon and the sirens would hurt their ears.

More cats disappeared. Geri Cook's white female named Snowball was let out for a ten o'clock stroll and didn't come home. Iris Hoblit's Smokey, an aggressive and sexually over-active tomcat, failed to return from an early morning outing.

Thinking it might lessen their desire for cat meat, we increased their rations. We threw them whole loaves of stale bread, ham bones, chicken breasts, slightly high veal, a salmon I had caught at April Point that had been in the freezer too long, quarts of ice cream with freezer burn.

One morning, we found remnants of what we had left out for the coyotes the night before. It had been picked up and put in a Gelson's shopping bag, and placed just on the inside of our white picket fence.

Attached to the bag was a scribbled note. "You're just encouraging them." The note was signed by Mr. Rhyder.

It was true. The coyotes had lost some of their caution, and had started appearing at our feeding station earlier and earlier each evening. Soon after our own dinner, we would go to the guest room and watch them take the food we had left for them.

The three-legged male would appear first, sneaking up through the avocado orchard, pausing at the edge of the road and, when he had determined that it was safe, he would cross to the feeding station. There he would make another judgment. When he was satisfied that the coast was clear, at some signal the female would arrive and cross to him. They ate quickly, gulping down the food, deserting it entirely if some car engine sounded down the road. They always heard the car before its lights appeared, and from our observation station we always marveled at their keen sense of hearing.

And then we had to go to Nashville for several weeks where I was producing the pilot for a new television series I had created for CBS. The series was about a young country and western singer named Boone whose ambition was to sing at the Grand Ole Opry and own a purple Cadillac.

In addition to indulging my love for country and western music, the series provided me two other very special pleasures. One was to stand on the same spot where Hank Williams sang among other classics, "I Can't Help It If I'm Still in Love with You." The other was to meet a lovely and cultivated woman named Minnie Pearl.

We worried about the coyotes while we were in Nashville, but the first night we were back, the coyotes were at our feeding station, and we noticed that while we had been away the female had grown fat. At first Jane and I made small jokes about what good providers we were, but then abruptly one night, we noticed that she had grown thin. When we caught sight of a swollen milk bag and teats, we realized with kind of a parental pride that she had given birth.

"I've got to start putting some vitamins in her food," observed Jane. A lot of people will say a thing like that for a joke, but she says it and means it.

I was curious about the size of the litter our female might have had. I did some research and discovered that the usual litter consists of six or eight pups, but that on occasion the female can deliver as many as eighteen or twenty. I also found out something we were to see borne out later. The male and female are monogamous and mate for life.

We watched from the guest house every night now, hoping they might bring their young with them, but they never did. Some nights the female did not arrive at all but after the male had satisfied his own hunger he would carry food off in his mouth. We supposed it was for his mate and the rest of the family.

One day Jane called me at my office.

"They're going to trap our coyotes," she said, her voice trembling with indignation.

"Who?" I asked.

"The Department of Animal Regulations. They're parked right across the street and they're carrying this awful-looking trap down into the avocado orchard."

"Tell them it could be dangerous to dogs," I said. "Tell them we object."

"I already did," she replied. "They just said if a dog gets in it they'll release it, and it's the kind of trap that doesn't hurt the animal."

"Tell them the coyotes are a family. Tell them they've got young pups to look after."

"I already did," she said. "They claim there isn't a thing they can do but follow orders."

"Sons of bitches!" I said.

"I told them that, too," said Jane.

"Tell them I'll get the law after them," I said.

"They are the law!" she said.

"You want me to come home?" I asked.

"There's nothing either one of us can do," said Jane. "It's just horrible and frustrating and I'm moving back to New York."

"I'll come with you," I said.

"Don't joke," said Jane. "Please, don't joke."

The trap became an overpowering presence in our lives. We did not speak of it, but I could see the worriment in Jane's eyes.

Privately I remembered a winter when I was a boy in Virginia and set out an old steel trap I had discovered in the barn. I baited it with an apple and set it down by Witt's Creek, my head reeling with the possibilities of the mink I would catch, the wealth I would realize from their pelts, and the ineffable excitement of visiting the trap each morning at first light.

For several of those boyhood days, the trap had not been visited. But then one morning as I approached, I saw that it had been tripped. The trap had remained secure to the ground where I had attached it, but the earth around it, in a perfect circle radiating from the center, had been scratched and clawed as some animal had fought desperately for its freedom. Finally, whatever I had trapped had taken the only alternative to capture it could know. It had bitten its way through its own leg and there in the trap, still marked by its teeth, was the small, padded, worn black-furred foot of a mink or a marten or a muskrat.

Sickened, I threw the trap and the amputated foot into the creek. I walked home filled with shame and despair that I had caused such pain to some creature, which at that very moment must be hidden, bleeding and in pain, in its den.

It was an experience that changed my life, and must in some mysterious way have led Jane and me to choose each other to be companions in life.

After the trap was set in the orchard, some nights the coyotes did not come to our feeding station at all. We reasoned that the trap had been set along their "run," that they were wary of it, and stayed away. We liked to believe that they would stay away and held on hopefully to our theory.

But then one night as we walked Yarrow on the road past the orchard, his fur rose, and we knew that something was amiss down there in the darkness.

I shone the light where Yarrow's stiffened pose indicated and there I saw the three-legged male coyote. He was digging frantically beside the trap the Animal Regulations people had set out, and there was something inside the trap.

Jane saw it, too.

"I'm going down there," she said.

I knew it would be useless to try to talk her out of it.

"Wait here," I said.

I walked Yarrow back to the house and locked him in the kitchen. He gave me that concerned, mildly troubled look he wears with me when he suspects I am going to do something foolish.

I then went back to join Jane where she waited at the

edge of the orchard. The bank down into the darkness was steep and overgrown with chaparral. I remembered thinking about rattlesnakes and wondering what I would do when we actually reached the cage.

There was no sign of the male coyote when we reached the cage, but inside was the female. She was quiet now, slinking down into the cage as far as she could get, as if she were trying to make herself as small as possible, trying not to be visible. The area all around the cage had been torn up, as if the male, in some way understandable only to him, had tried to dig his mate out of the cage. And when we shone the light into her face, her yellow eyes blazed with fear.

"What do we do now?" I asked Jane.

"We're going to let her go," said Jane with the calm and resolve she always exhibits during an emergency. (She falls apart later, but when we are in the eye of the storm, she keeps her wits about her.)

The captured coyote cringed deeper into the cage as we began examining the door to the trap. It turned out to be fastened with a simple release mechanism. We found it, pressed it, and the door dropped open. In that same moment the coyote sprang from the trap and melted into the darkness.

It had all happened so quickly that I am not sure either of us felt anything other than a quickening of breath and the faster beating of our hearts, but then, as we stood in front of the hateful trap and realized what we had done, we began to laugh. The sound of our laughter rose in volume until the coyotes themselves must have heard us in their den across the hill.

I think in that moment we shared an exultation that comes to few people. Perhaps those brave men and women who pilot their ships near whales that are being hunted by Japanese and Russians would know. Certainly we felt kinship with those who try to protect infant seals that are about to be clubbed to death for their fur. Perhaps, in that moment, our lives entwined with all those who see creatures both wild and human who are trapped, and who have conscience and concern and are moved to release them so they might live the fullest measure of their lives.

There are still coyotes in our neighborhood, children of old Three Foot and his lady. At dusk we hear their evensong. We don't feed them anymore, but we see them occasionally, silhouetted against the darkening sky, resting on their haunches for a moment's rest before going out to forage for the night.

18. That's No Rattlesnake!
That's My Alligator!

Nancy came into our lives in the winter of 1970. She was a small, wiry woman, an enemy of dirt and a treasure as a house cleaner. She distrusted us from the beginning, and was never really at ease with any of the family.

"That dog bite?" she asked the first day she came to work. She indicated Clemmentine, our blonde cocker spaniel. Clemmentine was elderly by then and almost incapable of biting even the mushy geriatric dog food we had to serve her, much less human flesh. We assured Nancy that Clemmentine was indeed harmless, but by this time the two of them had developed a mutual distrust that neither of them ever overcame.

"That one's got the devil in his eye," Nancy observed the first time she encountered Chloe. Nancy was right. Chloe was an ancient black female cocker spaniel who had always been odd. She spent the last years of her life hiding under Jane's bed. She would venture out only to relieve herself or when she might be hungry. At such time she would sprint for the backyard, or for her food bowl, a paranoid look in her eye, and a general deportment that seemed to suggest she was sure to be attacked unless she retreated under the bed again as quickly as possible. Chloe had been ill-tempered and hallucinatory from the time we had brought her home. But we accepted her with all her peculiarities and tried to make her as comfortable as possible.

"What does he do?" asked Nancy of Jane on her initial interview. She had a way of looking away from you and toward you at the same time, so it took me a moment to realize that the "he" she was referring to was me.

"He's a writer," said Jane with a degree of pride.

"What does he write?" asked Nancy, again ignoring my presence.

"He's written several scripts for *The Twilight Zone*," answered Jane.

"He take anything?" she asked.

"I don't understand," replied Jane.

"They take something," said Nancy. "Writing stuff like that, they must take something—or else they smoke that green stuff."

"He doesn't do that," said Jane.

"I hope not," said Nancy. "I'll be obliged to report it if I come across any. I don't as a rule work for people that smoke it."

We both assured her that neither of us smoked marijuana, but she didn't look for a moment convinced.

In spite of her apprehension about the dogs and my dope addiction, Nancy accepted the job of housekeeper. And she was superb. At the end of her day, the house would be immaculate. In the entire property there would not be a spider's web. Nowhere in the house could a speck of dust be found. The floors shined. The glassware sparkled. The sheets on the beds were taut and crisp. We looked for some imperfection, but none was there.

Nancy had worked for us only a short time before she became convinced that I was sexually overactive. I was a freelance writer in those days, working in an office at the foot of the hill on Ventura Boulevard. Often I would surprise Jane at midday and enjoy her company and the pleasure of a leisurely lunch at home.

When I came home for lunch the first time after Nancy started working for us, she hastily gathered up her cleaning equipment, whipped off her apron, and whispered to Jane, "I'll go wait in your car."

"Why?" asked Jane.

"I think he wants you-know," replied Nancy.

"Oh, no," replied Jane. "He's just home for lunch."

"That's what they said last place I worked," said Nancy. "I don't like to work for folks that do you-know at lunch."

And then she went and sat in Jane's car until I left the house. Nancy was a stubborn woman and we could never convince her that lunch and simply to enjoy Jane's company was really why I did come home from time to time, but I will confess that with Nancy sitting in the car, her fantasies would project themselves upon my mind, and I would indeed start thinking of you-know.

It was only when I had left the house that Nancy would return to finish her cleaning, but her fanciful conjecture about my sexual appetite was mild compared to her apprehensions about other residents at our house.

Jane had been feeding our peanut-loving blue jay on the deck at the kitchen door. With the smallest amount of encouragement, it would fly into the house. We had only to open the kitchen door to have the blue jay fly in and roost on the back of the yellow rocking chair. We had grown accustomed to its visits, and we accepted the bird as part of the natural order of things. But Nancy was unprepared, and the blue jay surprised her one morning on its usual visit in quest of peanuts.

We first became aware of the trouble the blue jay was causing when Nancy came out to the breakfast room and announced, "There's a chicken in the kitchen. It's a blue one and it's sitting on the back of that yellow chair like it owns the place."

"Oh," said Jane. "That's probably B. J."

I don't care what you call it," replied Nancy. "I don't work for people that keep chickens in their kitchens."

"It's not a chicken," said Jane. "It's a blue jay."

"It has pooped in three places," said Nancy, "and I know what chicken poop looks like because I was born in Texas. I never saw a blue one before, but I've seen a lot of things since I started here that I've never seen before."

Jane went to the kitchen and shooed the blue jay back

outdoors and I think there was a discussion about a small increase in salary if Nancy would remain on the job.

It is possible that Nancy might have remained with us indefinitely had it not been for Dale Remington.

We had met Dale Remington in the early New York years. He had recently arrived from Michigan and, like all of us recent arrivals, he was doing whatever he had to do to make a living. In Dale's case it meant he was impersonating a bunny rabbit in a window at Macy's.

But Dale was ambitious. Even though he enjoyed the job, he had no intention of spending the rest of his life impersonating a rabbit at Macy's. He moved from Macy's to NBC where he eventually landed on *The Tonight Show*. Eventually he started a business called Kaleidoscope, a company that filmed travelogues and documentaries.

And Dale traveled. We would know what part of the world he was in from the gifts that would arrive. A Masai mask told us he was in Africa. A sari arrived from India, a fly swatter from Egypt, a string of worry beads from Greece. But he also filmed in the United States and we gathered he had been filming in Florida when we received a six-inch-long alligator in the mail.

We determined to create a proper environment for it, but until we did, we made a home for it in the bathtub in the master bedroom.

In the frenzy of life on Avocado Drive, we forgot to mention to Nancy that a young alligator had taken up temporary residence in the bathroom.

Jane was dramatically reminded of her oversight the next day when Nancy came to clean. After dodging the "blue chicken" in the kitchen, Nancy moved to the bedroom and had managed to clean the room, and change the sheets, all the while dodging Chloe's menacing attacks from under the bed. It was only when Nancy went into the bathroom and came upon the alligator semi-submerged in the water, that she reached the point of no return.

Nancy ran screaming from the room. Without even collecting her cleaning equipment, she went to the garage and sat in Jane's car, a determined and resigned look on her face.

"It's all right, Nancy," said Jane, trying to reassure her that I was not expected on one of my lunchtime sexual raids.

"It's not him," she said.

"Then what's the matter?" asked Jane.

"I don't work for nobody that keeps rattlesnakes in their bathtubs," replied Nancy.

Jane drove her to the bus, and we never saw her again although we still receive a card from her at Christmas. It always features an animal and shows evidence of having been most carefully selected. As for the alligator, we gave him to the Los Angeles Zoo. He's a big fellow now, and if he knows us when we visit him, he shows no sign of recognition.

Dale Remington continues to travel around the world. When we last heard from him he was headed for China. And while we know it is improbable, we keep saying to each other: "A panda would be nice."

19. Family of 'Possums Disrupts Tranquil Garden of Zen!

Yarrow, our white Lab, stayed at home most of the time because he chose to. Had he wanted to go anywhere he had only to jump the fence and roam wherever he wished. Often he did leap over the fence and prowled the neighborhood for a sweetheart or for food or companionship. He had many friends and often went to visit the Hoblits or the Cooks or the Camberns. One morning when he disappeared for a brief time we did not worry, nor were we surprised a while later when he barked from down at the front gate. It was his signal that he was home again and wanted to be let back in the yard.

I was still at breakfast so Jane volunteered to go and open the gate. In a few minutes she called to me. I detected some distress in her voice.

"He's been hunting again!" Jane announced when I came to the foot of the stairs. She pointed to something small and wet on the driveway, which Yarrow was nosing.

"It's a baby 'possum and I think he's killed it," she said with an accusing look at Yarrow.

"Oh, Yarrow wouldn't harm a flea," I replied.

"You're just saying that because you're partial to him," she said.

"I said it because it's true."

I felt guilty because she was right. We tried not to play favorites with the dogs, but Jane was right. I was partial to Yarrow and loved him more than any other dog we had ever had.

"Please take that poor little dead thing away from him and bury it," said Jane.

I knelt to examine the dead 'possum. It was only about eight inches long. Its body consisted mostly of a long, naked rat-like tail. Its fur was mostly white and its small face tapered to a tiny pink nose, which was vulnerable and pathetic-looking. One of its ears had been nicked so that half of it was erect while the other half fell limply to the side. I hoped that Yarrow had not been rough with it.

The little animal was motionless. Its eyes were closed and its tongue lolled from its partially opened mouth. Saliva drooled from its lips to form a tiny wet spot on the concrete.

"This was a bad thing to do," I said to Yarrow. I hated to scold him because he was a sensitive dog and could sense our feelings often without our expressing them.

"Sit," I instructed him, trying my best to sound stern.

Yarrow obediently moved back from his "kill" and sat, waiting for further instructions. I knelt to get a better look at the 'possum. As I came closer I detected just the faintest movement around its tiny nostrils.

"I think this little guy is playing 'possum," I announced. Jane was not convinced so to prove my point I gently nudged it with the toe of my shoe. The possum showed no reaction.

"If it wasn't dead before it is now, kicking it that way," observed Jane.

"I have never kicked an animal in my life," I objected.

"What about that pigeon you said you kicked in Central Park?"

"That was a bird!" I explained. "And I didn't intend to kick that pigeon. I thought it was going to move out of my way."

"It's that hunter-gatherer culture you come from," she sniffed. "Ready to shoot anything that moves!"

It seemed the wrong time to point out that my hunter-gatherer forebears most of the time afforded food for the table by shooting it.

"I'm going to put this 'carcass' in the cat carrier, and you watch my word. It will be alive in an hour or so."

I put on a glove and lifted the little body into the cat carrier that we had stored in the bins in the garage. If it was playing 'possum it was doing a convincing job because it felt limp and cold and dead. We opened the gate to let Yarrow back in the yard and returned to breakfast.

We had left the cat carrier in the garage. On my way to work I glanced at it. There clinging to the side of the wire cage, very much alive, and most inquisitive-looking was the possum. She had given up her dead pose and looked not only alive, but hungry.

The injured ear with its half-erect, half-floppy nature gave her face an almost comical appearance.

"She would like an apple," I said to Jane when I returned to the kitchen.

"Would she like a Starks Delicious or a Winesap?" asked Jane sarcastically.

In spite of her facetious attitude Jane was the first to get to the cage. She was still feeding bits of apple, onion, carrots, and Black Forest ham through the opening in the cage when I left for work.

"No caviar?" I asked.

"It's not good for them," she said as she shot me an annoyed look.

"She's kind of cute, isn't she?" I observed.

"We're not going to keep her," Jane insisted. "We've got enough wildlife to look after already."

The thought had only faintly crossed my mind.

That evening when I came home from work I took the cat carrier down to the avocado orchard and lifted the trap door. I expected the 'possum to make an exit, but it refused to leave the container. Whether it was afraid to go, or liked it there, or it failed to realize that freedom was so close at hand I could not tell. Finally I tipped the carrier over on its side and shook it. The 'possum clung to the wire sides of the cage for a moment and suddenly let go and went running off into the orchard.

I did not think of the baby 'possum for quite some time. I had become preoccupied with a new project. Ever since Jane and I visited Japan I had longed for a Japanese garden.

Unfortunately our yard had already been designed with old-fashioned annual borders, a rose garden for Jane and a vegetable patch for me. There was not really a place for my dream of a Japanese garden.

And then one day I was staring at a strip of hillside between the pool deck and Avocado Drive. It was a narrow shaded area where some old lumber had been rotting for years. On top of the lumber was stored a length of galvanized pipe, two rusted tomato cages, and some discarded plastic pots. I was wondering how the area's appearance could be improved when suddenly I envisioned a carpet of baby's tears leading to a Japanese stone lantern. Tastefully planted in the center of a little island of white gravel was a black pine tree trimmed and trained as a bonsai. A small koi pond, where water lilies blossomed, bordered a grouping of river stones suggestive of the tips of mountains. In my imagination a fountain rose from the center of the koi pond providing a sweet mist to the air and the cooling sound of water gurgling over moss-covered stones. Over the entire landscape was a sense of serenity and harmony and beauty.

The garden did not turn out quite as harmonious as I had envisioned it, but it was an addictive and fun activity. Working early mornings before going to work and on weekends, gathering the materials, shopping for plants at lunch, and finally doing the actual planting were a pleasure. The work went on for over a year before I placed a votive candle in the stone lantern, and sat down one evening just after sundown to contemplate my Zen garden.

In the light of the stone lantern the garden appeared just about the way I had imagined it. The baby's tears had taken vigorous hold and had spread enthusiastically. In place of a large koi pond I had sunk a whiskey barrel in the ground, planted a water lily in it and stocked it with goldfish.

A portion of the garden could be seen from the street and often when I was meditating there a neighbor would stop to gossip or supervise or admire my handiwork.

One of those who stopped most often was my neighbor from up the road, the gentleman from the Department of Animal Regulations, who had objected so strongly to my keeping a rooster. When he stopped he would peer suspiciously behind me as if to assure himself that I was not breaking some animal regulation. I toyed with the idea of semi-concealing a cutout of a Bengal tiger in the foliage behind me just to confirm his suspicion. I mentioned the notion to Jane but she discouraged me, claiming that it might inflame him further.

Today his mind was on law enforcement.

"It's those damn illegal aliens!" he fumed.

"What have they done now?" I asked, for I had heard his views on this subject before.

"They're hiding out down in the orchard," he complained

He had probably seen some gardener tending to his legitimate business, but I knew it would do no good to try to convince him of that.

"You keep your gun handy?" he wanted to know.

I had to confess that I did not own a gun. From my army

training I knew how to handle everything from a .45 to an M-1 rifle, but I had never felt the need to own a gun in civilian life.

Mr. Rhyder clucked with disapproval and went on up the road. A short while later he returned and handed me an object. It was a long narrow pouch made of leather. It was very heavy, with a stout thong at one end.

"It's a sap," he explained. "All it is is a piece of buckskin filled with birdshot. You wake up in the middle of the night with some illegal alien looking you in the eye, you just haul this sweetheart from under your pillow and smash his damn face in!"

Solemnly I promised to do that. Mr. Rhyder left to go about the business of protecting our street from illegal aliens, but it took some time for the serenity and harmony of my garden to be restored.

Serenity and harmony were disturbed in time by another caller. This one was a stranger, and I suspected a four-legged one. The carpet of baby's tears was torn up and tossed in clumps about the area. My Japanese stone lantern had been tilted so that it looked more like the leaning tower of Pisa. My azaleas had been uprooted and left to die, and my stones, which had been selected and placed to resemble the tips of mountains, looked like mounds of mud. Something had reached into the lily pond and pulled out the lilies. The gold fish were so spooked they lurked in the deepest part of the whiskey barrel.

I suspected that the intruder had been a four-footed animal. Being an old country boy I began looking for footprints and I found them. Two small prints in the mud were formed like stars. They were followed by other tracks consisting of a thumb-like toe, three middle toes spaced close together, and a fifth somewhat smaller toe. From my career as a trapper when I was ten years old I recognized 'possum.

On the third night after the incident I set out the Havaheart Trap. As its name implies it does not harm the trapped animal. I was delighted to trap the intruder, an opossum. And when I examined her more closely I recognized from her deformed ear that she was the same animal Yarrow had brought home when she was a baby. She was grown now, a fat and sassy adult. This time she did not feign death but hissed at me and bared her teeth in a threatening gesture.

Jane and the children were at the beach. When I called Jane to tell her that I had captured a 'possum and that I was going to release her Jane instructed me to give her a good square meal before letting her go.

I placed the trap with the 'possum in it in the potting shed, dumped in grapes, leftover steak, lettuce, a croissant with a glob of peanut butter in it, and a tomato and cucumber salad. I filled the water bowl and ignored her hisses and threats and went to work. That evening I approached the trap quietly hoping to surprise my captive. I did, and I also was in for a surprise. She was not alone. On her prehensile tail she was supporting five of her children, each of them as small as she herself had been the day that Yarrow had brought her home.

I should have released her that evening, but I was curious

about her family. I wanted to watch them and see how they related to her and to one another. I wondered if they ever returned to their mother's pouch the way a young kangaroo will return to its kangaroo pouch. If the 'possums ever did, I did not see it happen.

A heat wave came, one of those desert scorchers that bake the earth and singe the leaves of trees and beds of ivy. I felt that the weather was much too hot to release the 'possum family into the wild. So I kept them. My family had fled to the beach and in their absence the 'possums provided a presence waiting when I came home from work. In the dog's absence they gave me something to feed and to care for. I told myself that it was the blistering weather that kept me from letting them go, but in truth I enjoyed looking after them. I learned that they were partial to fish and I began buying cans of anchovies for them.

Finally the weather turned cool and I no longer had any excuse to keep them captive. I took them down into the orchard where I had released the mother so long ago. She lifted her tail with her youngsters clinging to it and shuffled off into the underbrush.

Mr. Rhyder was on an errand the next time he stopped.

"Just wanted to tell you not to let your dog wander," he said.

"This place is overrun with predators lately. I had one of my boys put out some poison down in the orchard."

"I wish you hadn't done that," I replied. "I hate to see an animal suffer."

"Oh they don't suffer," he answered. "It hits their blood stream and they just kind of explode."

As soon as Mr. Rhyder left I went down in the orchard and searched for the poison, but "his boys" had done their job well and I met with no success. All week the vision of the mother opossum and her children exploding haunted me, and I resolved to try to catch them before they got into the poison.

I set out the Havaheart Trap again, baited it with anchovies, apples, grapes, and any aromatic leftovers I could find in the refrigerator.

Each morning I went out to see if I had caught anything. Eventually, over a period of time, I caught three of them. None of them were the mother, but I like to think they were her children.

Once an animal has been caught in a trap they learn not to enter it again. Perhaps the mother had become cautious and elected not to be seduced by my bait.

Each of the ones I caught I took far from Avocado Drive. There is a rustic area above Azusa in the San Gabriel Mountains. A picturesque stream, which is stocked with trout, tumbles down the mountain. Families who go there to picnic often leave food scraps behind. Fishermen leave bait and bits of sandwiches.

I still keep the trap set and baited. Each time I catch another 'possum I take it to the mountains and release it. The menu there is not quite as fancy as what Jane and I provide, but at least the animals are alive and in no danger from being poisoned.

Mr. Rhyder passed away not long ago, but I still have the sap he gave me. If any aliens, illegal or otherwise, ever decide to sneak up on me in the night they had better watch their step!

20. The Cat Who Loved the Liver and Cheese Medley!

I have never liked cats. They seem to know I don't like them and seem not to care much for me either. It was therefore something of a shock to me when I met and became fond of a cat named Surprise.

I know how my distrust of cats began. When I was growing up in the Blue Ridge Mountains of Virginia the cats I came in contact with were wild and predatory. They earned an honest living catching rats and mice in the barn. They were not pets. They were working animals and life, as it was for most of us during the Great Depression, was lean and chancy.

Growing up in the rural South I inherited superstitions that had been handed down for generations. One of them was that you should never go to sleep in the same room with a cat, for the cat was sure to wait until you were asleep then suck out your breath!

I believed it then, and to be absolutely honest, I am still uneasy if I have to sleep in a room with a window opened wide enough for a cat to enter. I may be on the fortieth floor of a hotel, but if the window is opened just enough for a cat to squeeze through you can be sure that it is closed before I go to bed. You just never know when they will sneak up on you.

Black cats crossing the road ahead of my car are worrisome. I know that it will only be a matter of time before it will bring me bad luck. At the same time I tell myself that to believe in such superstitions is a shameful evidence of ignorance. But no matter what I tell myself, if a black cat crosses the road ahead of me, I break into a cold sweat, my heart begins to race, and I find myself making a U-turn and looking for an alternate route.

And yet a fine relationship developed between me and a black cat that came to live with us on Avocado Drive.

He received the name Surprise because he simply showed up one morning. He appeared at the back door unannounced. He was a surprise.

This kind of thing was happening more and more frequently. I suspect the reputation of the Hamners, the Cooks, the Camberns, and the Hoblits for being animal freaks was becoming well known. More and more, Avocado Drive was becoming a dumping ground for animals nobody else wanted or could no longer care for.

From time to time I'd find an apprehensive-looking dog waiting at the front gate when I went down to get the morning paper. They gave me the feeling that their former owners had left them there with instructions to try to appear pathetic until we took pity on them and gave them a home. There had been more cats than we could count, a family of parrots, and most bizarre of all, a monkey-like animal, which is still spotted every three months or so. The monkey does not seem so much to be looking for a home as he does to be enjoying his freedom. He is affectionately referred to as "Smallfoot."

There was absolutely nothing appealing about the cat that came to be known as Surprise. He was thin and he had no hair on his tail. His abdominal region was sunken, his coat was an unlikely gunmetal blue and spots of scabby white skin showed through his thin fur. He had a scrappy look, as if he were descended from hillbillies.

If there was anything that set Surprise aside from any other stray cat it was an air of determination, a visible will and need to survive. I had seen it in the eyes of children of the Depression, and later in children of wartime Europe, and I knew it for what it was.

It was that look which made me take a wait-and-see attitude with the cat on our first encounter. Neither of us made an overture. We were neither friends nor enemies, but we each watched the other warily, and then he ran off into the chaparral, and I forgot all about him.

Soon after this, something began moving about under the house at night. I was wakened more than once by the sound of small footsteps, or the faint rustle of paper. I mentioned it to Jane, and she said, "I remember now why it was I swore I would never marry a Southerner."

"And why was that?" I demanded.

"Ghosts," she said. "Your mothers teach you all those spooky things."

"This is no spook," I shouted. "It's something alive and it moves about all night long down there—and you leave my mother out of this!"

"You know perfectly well I have nothing but admiration for your mother, and I don't see why you brought her into this in the first place."

"I didn't," I hollered. "You did."

Jane looked at me and giggled. "Are we having a fight?"

"Yes," I said indignantly. "It's a fight."

"I forget how it started," she said.

"You attacked my mother," I said.

"Now I remember," she said. "You're afraid of that noise under the house."

"It has nothing to do with my mother," I objected.

"Of course not," she replied. "Whatever gave you such an idea?"

After a week or so, I discovered that Surprise was living under the house. He had gained access through a screened crawl space that I had not repaired since a dog named Sandy had torn the screen away years ago.

Even though I knew the cat was close by, and that I could die almost any night from suffocation, I felt reasonably safe if I took precautions. I took care to close my windows at night and was also sure that the door to my room was fully closed. Sometimes I would get up in the middle of the night to check the windows and doors, for I never forget that it was possible that I would waken some night and find that the cat had somehow gained access to my bedroom and that my breath was being sucked away.

"Don't feed it," I warned Jane. "Maybe it will go to somebody else's house."

"Of course I'm going to feed it," she replied. "It's hungry!"

Once she began feeding the cat it was no longer "the" cat, but "our" cat.

As she usually did with a new animal, Jane went through a period when she would get to know the newcomer. Within a short time she would know its phobias, its delusions, likes and dislikes regarding bedding materials, preferred time to wake up or go to sleep, as well as its food preference.

"Don't give Surprise the 'Sea-Food Delight,'" she would instruct me if I were home alone and the feeding chores fell to me.

"Why not?" I would ask.

"He loves the 'Liver and Cheese Medley' and he really goes crazy if you pour a little brown gravy over it."

"Are you sure he wouldn't prefer a little beluga caviar?"

"I've never tried it," she answered, "but you can if you want to give him a special treat."

Gradually, perhaps due to the carefully balanced meals Jane was feeding him, Surprise began changing color. His coat began to turn a richer, deeper hue. The white sores that had been visible through his fur became less and less angry and eventually disappeared altogether. His fur turned from a sickly blue to gray to a darker shade of gray until the day arrived when we had to admit that we had a black cat on our hands.

Except for an occasional feeding, there had been few encounters between Surprise and me. With most of the pets, I would call out a greeting when I passed them. "Hey, Yarrow! How's it hanging?" "Yo, Sandy! Let's go catch a 'possum!" Or something equally clever. Usually the dog I addressed with such jocularity would return a look that acknowledged that I was being silly. Surprise and I shared no such familiarity.

One day I found him inching his way along a limb of the walnut tree in the backyard. He was not far from the branch of a tree that housed a family of nesting doves.

Doves are among the least able architects in existence. Their nests, even the most sporty, can consist of two or three crossed twigs. The more expansive models, which is to say those boasting such luxuries as linings of cotton balls or feathers or an extra twig to add to the stability of the structure, are rare. It is not unusual to discover the undeveloped fetus of a baby dove, already dead or only half alive, too soon fallen from the nest, gasping for air and life and sustenance somewhere underneath the poorly constructed nursery. That doves are able to raise their families to maturity is something of a miracle considering the housing problem.

When I came across Surprise sneaking along the tree limb toward the doves' nest, I surmised he was bent on murder so

I grabbed the hose and sprayed him generously with cold water. He leaped from the tree, came to rest in the ivy bed and gave me a look of the purest hatred. I did not see him for several days and when I did, he refused to look at me.

That was to be our relationship for some time to come. I would arrive home from work to find him resting on the limb of the walnut tree that reached out above the kitchen door. He would observe me with an even look, all the while lashing his tail about in a defiant way as if to say that he knew that Jane was home and that she would protect him if I tried anything.

And then the rats came.

There was a shelf at the back door where I stored garden supplies such as fertilizer and trowels and pruning shears. Forgotten at the rear of the shelf was a roll of paper towels. On my annual cleaning I removed all the gardening equipment and was reaching for the roll of paper towel when a large rat came careening off the shelf. When I went inside to get a flashlight so as to be sure it was safe to stick my hand back in the shelf, Jane asked what I was up to.

"We've got rats," I announced.

"I know," she said. "There's a whole nest of them. I think there are nine in all."

"My God," I said. "An army of rats."

"I was afraid you would find them," she said with a sigh.

"Why were you afraid I'd find them?" I asked.

"Because you'll probably want to do something awful to them."

"I think we have to get rid of them. Yes," I said.

"How?"

"With a stick, a baseball bat, something I can squash them with."

"Don't you dare squash them with anything!" she warned.

"Jane, they are rodents," I said emphatically.

"I don't care what you call them, you're not going to kill them."

"Somebody has to do it," I said. "They are pests. They bite and they carry diseases and they multiply faster than rabbits!"

By this time we had reached the back porch. With Jane beside me I shone the flashlight toward the back of the shelf. There on a pile of shredded paper towel was a squirming mass of little red hairless bodies with tiny red squiggly tails.

"I could gas them," I said. "They'd never feel a thing."

"I can't believe you would do such a thing," she said. "Sometimes I think I don't know you at all."

"I suppose next thing we know you'll be setting a place for them at the table," I said sarcastically, "inviting them in the TV room to watch *Murphy Brown*, or taking them to the Ivy to dinner."

"No," she said, "but when they get big enough, I am going to set out a humane trap and when they are all in it I am going to take them someplace where they will be safe and can live out their lives. In the meantime, I am going to set out some milk for the mother. It must be a terrible strain to nurse that many babies."

When I closed the door to the cabinet, something happened to catch my attention from the overhanging limb of the Chinese elm. Surprise was there, and his tail was lashing back and forth with the greatest excitement.

In time the little naked red blobs in the paper towel nest grew to be an appealing family of rather handsome young rats. There were not nine, but twelve of them, young, quick, fawn-colored little four-legged motors that would dart out from under the shelf to the bird feeder. There they would grasp a single seed and then hastily retreat underneath the deck to enjoy their meal.

As entertaining as they were to watch, I knew that the time would come when they would overrun our small property—and then the entire San Fernando Valley and quite possibly most of southern California—unless somebody broke their reproductive cycle.

Now that the young rats were large enough to be captured and transported somewhere else, Jane started looking for a Havaheart Trap. At a tack and feed shop in Burbank she located one, but it was meant for animals the size of opossums and raccoons.

The rats grew bold. The bird feeder became their playground. They no longer grabbed a seed and darted back to their hiding place. They sat in the bowl of the feeder and gnawed away to their hearts content. I even imagined that if the bird food was depleted they sat and looked our direction in an aggrieved way, but Jane said my imagination was working overtime again.

I suggested rat poison.

"You just don't understand," objected Her Majesty. "Those rats' lives are just as precious to them as mine is to me. Taking a life, any life, is murder as far as I'm concerned! Just give me time to find the right trap and I'll get rid of them."

It was then that Surprise stepped in.

We woke one morning to find a dead rat at the back door. When I went out to remove it, Surprise was watching. I picked up the rat by its tail and tossed it out into the yard. Surprise pounced on the carcass, picked it up, brought it back and laid it at my feet. I threw it out to him again, and this time he grabbed the rat and tossed it in the air several times. He then brought it to me as if inviting me to enjoy the sport. I didn't accept his invitation, but I did pet him and recognized a friend.

Every morning thereafter there was a gift from Surprise at the back door. At first Jane threatened to move to London, but instead she continued looking for a Havaheart Trap. By the time she found one of the right size, Surprise had diminished the rat population considerably, but she did manage to trap the last three of them. By now they were adults of such size and audacity that they swaggered confidently around the patio at all hours of the day.

We released them in the Los Angeles National Forest and if anyone missed them it was Surprise. He stayed with us for quite a long time, but then one morning he was gone and we never saw him again. We think probably a coyote got him.

21. Odd Couple Cohabit in Garden. Tragic Results from Encounter with Famous Actor's Dog!

Raymond and George lived together in a cage in the far corner of the garden. They were just two members of the Avocado Drive Zoo who lived on with us after Scott and Caroline went away to college. Raymond was a white male rabbit and George was a multicolored guinea pig. Raymond's eyes were pink and the way they were set in his face gave him a shy, endearing appearance. The pattern of George's orange and white fur gave his face a devil-may-care expression.

Each of the animals had family backgrounds. Raymond had fathered numerous litters of young rabbits. With the exception of the times when he had either eaten or kicked to death a good many of the litter, he had been a model head of the family. George, the guinea pig, had also been an attentive and devoted father and husband.

The rabbit and the guinea pig were widowed at about the same time. For a while they lived alone in separate cages, and then Jane and I decided that the time had come to consolidate. We wanted to cut back on the space taken up by the zoo and to return the backyard to grass and flowers. That was when we placed the rabbit and the guinea pig together in a single cage.

At first they circled each other warily. Occasionally Raymond would leap into the air, often turning a somersault while airborne. The guinea pig did no such tricks but made alarmed whistling sounds and cringed fearfully against the side of the cage.

Within a few days their distrust of each other seemed to subside. Raymond would still leap into the air from time to time, but now he seemed to be showing off for George rather than threatening him. Raymond's whistle began to sound less alarmed and a bit throaty, with a suggestion of lasciviousness in it. The first we discovered that a friendship had developed was on our nightly inspection when we found the rabbit and the guinea pig asleep. They were stretched out companionably beside each other as if they enjoyed the closeness. We began calling them "The Odd Couple."

There was a German shepherd in the neighborhood who used to go past our house every night. He was an enormous dog with silver tinted black-tipped fur, beautiful to look at but unsettling to meet on the quiet road after the sun went down.

The dog belonged to a Famous Actor who lived down the road from us. I have never known the actor and as events evolved it turned out to be just as well.

There came a time when some animal gained access to our backyard and was disturbing the livestock while we slept. Some mornings we would find small cages overturned and footsteps trailing through the dewy grass. We suspected the German shepherd from the very first.

One night I decided to stay up and keep vigil. I sat quietly beside the outdoor grill and waited for whatever might appear. I was nearly ready to leave my outpost when a huge, furry shape leaped over the chain link fence from above the fish pond and came crashing down across the ivy embankment.

I recognized the German shepherd and waited to see what he would do. He went directly to the cage and began pawing at the chicken wire that separated him from the rabbit and the guinea pig. I could not see them, but I could imagine the two harmless old bachelors cringing against each other for security and comfort.

Once I was sure it was the shepherd that was disturbing the zoo, I broke from my hiding place and went running toward him shouting in a loud voice. The dog looked at me more with impatience than in fear, then leaped over the lower wall where the African daisies grew, and went running off toward the Famous Actor's home.

It was not the last of his visits. I found him in our yard time and time again. Our odd couple seemed to be of special interest to him. Often I would discover him sitting and staring into the cage, totally preoccupied with the rabbit and the guinea pig. At other times he would do his best to break into the cage by pawing at the wire. Whenever I interrupted his raids, I would run and shout at him, throwing a beer can, a rake, a flowerpot, whatever came to hand. He would give me an insolent look then disappear over the bank.

One night I went out to check on the wildlife. When I came to the odd couple's cage I found it overturned, their water dish empty, their food dish on its side. The wire had been clawed away and neither the rabbit nor the guinea pig was anywhere in sight.

I searched around the yard. I looked under the gardenia bush where in the moonlight a luminous, cabbage-like, heavily perfumed blossom shown at the end of each stem. The corner of the camellia bed where the hose connection was broken, leaving a constant supply of running water for any thirsty wild or tame thing, was empty of life. There was no sign of them under the deck at the back door, not even of the elderly female opossum that occasionally sought refuge there. I continued looking until Jane came to the back door and called:

"What's going on?"

"Nothing," I lied. Even though there had been no sign of either animal, I felt there was a chance I might find one of them before I went to bed and there would be no reason to distress Jane with what could well be a false alarm.

"I'm taking my shower," she said and disappeared into the house.

"I'll be along," I called.

I figured that the villain was very probably the Famous Actor's dog and that if I hurried, I might make it to the Famous Actor's house, investigate the crime and quite possibly retrieve the rabbit or the guinea pig from the marauding dog and be back by the time Jane finished her shower.

The house was in darkness. There was no sign of the German shepherd, although once I touched the doorbell, the howls of a dog from hell began to sound from somewhere inside the house.

Finally a slash of light at the foot of the door coincided with the sound of a female voice.

"Who's there?" called the wife of the Famous Actor.

"Earl Hamner," I called, trying modestly to keep a note of self-importance out of my voice. After all, I was the Creator and Executive Producer of *The Waltons*, the number one rated television series in the country. Surely someone who lived only a few houses away would be aware that she had a neighbor of such distinction.

"Who?" she called.

"One of your neighbors," I shouted, trying to keep the indignation out of my voice.

"What do you want?" she called.

"I think your dog may have made off with my rabbit," I said.

Silence from beyond the door.

"My guinea pig is missing, too," I said.

Imagine opening the door in the middle of the night to a

strange man complaining that his rabbit had been disturbed and that his guinea pig was missing! To the credit of the wife of the Famous Actor, she opened the door and looked out cautiously.

"Who did you say you are?"

"Earl Hamner," I replied, lowering my voice modestly.

"Oh," she said. "I think the children watch your show on television."

What discerning children she must have, I thought. What a responsibility we television celebrities carry! To think that only a few doors from where I lived, young lives were being molded and bent by words I had written! Their characters were being formed by me. Their future was in my hands!

"They wrote to your star once," she said. "He didn't write back."

"Richard always answers his fan mail," I said, stoutly defending the star of my series. "I'm sure if the letter reached him he would have answered it."

"I don't know who Richard is," she said. "It was Michael Landon they wrote to and asked for his autograph."

I realized that the children of the Famous Actor were fans not of *The Waltons*, but of another television series called *The Little House on the Prairie*.

Not only had their savage dog raided my yard and made off with one or more of our pets, but they didn't even know that they lived down the street from such a distinguished citizen as the creator of *The Waltons*!

"You keep that dog home from now on," I said in my forceful Executive Producer voice.

"The dog never leaves home," she said and gently but firmly closed the door.

On my way home I encountered Jane. She was fresh from her shower and had come looking for me to tell me that she had just discovered that the rabbit and the guinea pig were missing.

"There's nothing we can do," I said. "Not tonight."

"There's lots more to be done," she said.

"Like what?" I asked.

"We're gong to find them," she said. I had heard that tone of voice before. I knew there would be no sleep until we located them.

We searched together for a long time. We followed the old road past the elm tree as far as the grown-over foliage would allow us to go. At one point we came upon the fat old female 'possum that often sought refuge under our deck. Tonight she was sitting on her haunches in the moonlight and eating a fresh peach, which she held in her paws and nibbled at with the greatest delicacy.

"Go home, you old fool," scolded Jane. "It's dangerous to be out tonight."

"It's dangerous for us to be out here, too," I said to Jane.

"You can go to bed if you want to," she replied. "I'm going to keep looking."

At the intersection of Cinco and Avocado where the road branched, I followed Cinco and Jane continued along

Avocado Drive. The time was nearing one o'clock when I came upon a strange spot in the middle of the road. In the moonlight it appeared to be a shimmering white pool. A tiny star might have fallen there and exploded, leaving shreds of residual light. It was like nothing I had ever seen before.

But then I knelt and touched the edge of the white pool. It was cool and silken and damp to the touch. When I brought my fingers up to my face I could see that they had touched white fur. Whatever had violated our yard had taken our white rabbit off to this spot and had shaken it to death.

I resolved not to tell Jane. The news seemed too bizarre, too cruel at that late hour to tell to someone who had loved the rabbit. I would tell her in the morning; I would show her the spot in the sunlight when the sun dispelled the grotesqueness of the silken white pool of fur. I would pro-tect her.

And I made a mistake. I misjudged my wife.

When I caught up with her, I suggested we abandon the search and turn in for the night.

"I can't sleep as long as they are out here lost," she said. "You go on to sleep. I'm going to keep looking."

I knew she wasn't going to discontinue her search, and there was no way I could go to sleep thinking of her alone out there at night finding that pathetic pool of white fur. So I led her to it and showed her what I had discovered.

I had expected distress, tears even. Instead she turned to me angrily.

"Why didn't you show me this right away?" she demanded.

"I didn't want to upset you," I answered.

"It upsets me even more that you don't think I can deal with this kind of thing."

"I wanted to spare you the pain," I replied.

"Next time try sharing the pain," she said, and at that moment our marriage took an entirely new and healthy direction toward trust and maturity in which I felt free to readily share not just the good news but that which could be uncomfortable to receive.

The Famous Actor's German shepherd did not come around again. Perhaps his owners kept him fenced in. And after a little while the family moved away altogether. What became of the guinea pig we never did find out.

22. The Arrival and Departure of Sandy!

He was the most pathetic-looking dog I had ever seen. He stood by our front gate, not even asking to be let in, but simply requesting not to be driven away. He looked as if he would be grateful if only to be allowed some place to rest for the night.

I noticed him as I drove into the garage, a large unkempt mongrel. The expression "hangdog" might have been coined just for him. He was thin and gaunt and his coat was matted and dirty. He appeared poised for flight at any moment and he observed me warily as I got out of the car and walked past him to the gate. He was collie mostly, but with a variety of other breeds mixed in. The reddish-brown coat was tipped with black, his eyes were the near-human eyes of Labradors, his ears could have been German shepherd, and there looked to be even a little coyote in him. Mostly he just looked tired and hungry.

"There's a hungry dog down at the gate," I announced as I walked into the kitchen. Within seconds Jane had opened a can of dog food, emptied it onto a paper plate and was on her way out the door.

"What about our cocktails?" I called after her.

"Bring them down to the gate." She is usually a bit rigid about the social graces, but all reason deserts her in the presence of anything hungry, especially if it is homeless, four-footed, and furry.

I mixed the champagne cocktail Jane always enjoys before dinner, poured myself a generous glass of chardonnay and carried them down to the gate. Jane was sitting on the top of the brick steps watching the stray dog. He was licking up the last of the canned food and seemed to be considering eating the paper plate as well.

"He's been abandoned," said Jane. "He hasn't eaten in days and he's been in a fight."

"He told you all that?" I asked.

"I just know," she said.

"We can't keep him," I announced firmly.

"It never crossed my mind," lied Jane, "but we can leave the garage door open tonight and let him get a good night's sleep."

"Sensible," I said. I knew it would be useless to object.

"And there's an old blanket I've been meaning to throw away. We'll put that down and make it more comfortable for him." The dog was already looking at her with something just a hair short of adoration. "He'll probably be gone by morning."

"I'm sure," I replied.

Before she went to bed, Jane took water and a midnight snack down to the dog. The following morning he was, of course, still there.

"I should take him to the pound right now," I said. "If he stays around here you're going to get to liking him and pretty soon we'll have another dog on our hands."

"I'll take him to the pound later on this afternoon," she promised. "I just want to treat that infected ear first. It looks as if it got torn in the fight."

I was away from home often in those days because I was producing a television series for CBS that I had also created, *Falcon Crest* starring Jane Wyman. It was necessary to make frequent trips to the Napa Valley where we did location shooting. This time I was away for a month.

By the time I returned home, the torn ear had healed, and the dog had acquired the name Sandy, his own doghouse on the patio, and a shiny new coat, the result of a daily brushing and excellent nutrition.

From the beginning, Sandy was an erratic dog. Some days he was as gentle as Lassie, affectionate, obedient, and calm. On other days the coyote in him came out, and he became cunning. He hated the whole tribe of cats. He could sneak up on a cat without its knowing he was nearby, and more than once nearly caught one in his mouth. It was the same with birds, and he took great pleasure out of inching his way up to a dove, then nosing it, and watching the stupid bird catapult into the sky.

Almost immediately he assumed the role of watchdog and would bark and bare his teeth ferociously at any person who even dared come near the front gate. But his ferocity was all for show. If anyone dared advance toward him and raise a stick or their voice, like the Cowardly Lion, Sandy would retreat to any place where he could hide his embarrassment.

He was a wanderer. We tried tying him up at night, but he refused to stay tied. He would stretch the rope as far as it would go, then throw his weight against it until the rope broke, or until he had dragged the doghouse to which he was attached halfway to Sacramento. Often he would be gone much of the night, returning at daylight, tired and sleepy and hungry. We suspected he had been accepted into the local pack of coyotes and spent his nights roaming the hills with them.

Sandy was one of the few dogs we had who seemed to like me almost as much as he liked Jane. He always came to meet me when I arrived home from work; he loved to ride in my car; and if he knew I was going for a walk he had to go with me. It was unusual to have a dog in the family who preferred to sleep at my feet rather than Jane's, and that endeared him to me.

He was an ardent lover. When Felice, the Camberns' German shepherd, came in heat, Don and Pat, being proper pet owners, kept her in the house. This deterred Sandy only temporarily. No matter how we tried to confine him to our yard, he would get out and circle the Cambern property, studying the situation, waiting in case Felice might find her way out to him. When none of his stratagems worked he took action. Somehow he leaped through the kitchen window without killing himself, and was having his way with Felice when Pat came to investigate the crash. Once again we had reason to be thankful for understanding and indulgent neighbors.

The indulgence of some of our other neighbors was put to the test when Sandy developed a hatred for Flo. Flo was a female calico cat that belonged to Iris Hoblit who lives up the hill directly east of us. Iris and Fred Hoblit are the kind of people who upon learning your car battery is dead, appear with cables, a battery jumper, and a fully charged car battery. If you go away for a weekend or a month or a year, Iris and Fred will feed your fish or your chicken or your cat. Iris is an absolutely fearless person. She thinks nothing of walking into the middle of deadly traffic on Ventura Boulevard to rescue a runaway dog. I have even seen her wade into the middle of a dog fight, pull the combatants away from each other and hold them apart until their owners arrived or until the angry tempers simmered down.

Flo liked to tease Sandy. She would position herself not too far from him, sit, and start cleaning herself as if she were unaware of Sandy's presence. Sandy would go into his coyote act and hunker down flat and inch himself as close as he could get to her. Finally he would spring, jaws agape, only to find that he had landed on an empty space and that Flo was sitting on a tree limb laughing down at him.

It used to drive him crazy.

And then one day, Flo grew jaded with the game, got too sure of herself, or maybe she just underestimated Sandy. He caught her!

As if to say, "Look, I won the game!" Sandy brought Flo to the back door and handed her to Jane. Flo was very much alive, and she struggled, but she was deeply wounded in her abdominal region. Together, Jane and Iris rushed Flo to Dr. Garner.

Dr. Garner took Flo into his examining room and came out a short time later.

"She won't be having any more kittens," he said.

"What's that got to do with anything?" asked Iris.

"Sandy gave her one of the neatest hysterectomies I've ever seen," said the doctor.

We never knew Sandy's exact age because we were never sure just how old he was when he came to us. But Dr. Garner guessed him to be three or four years old when he arrived and he had been with us for ten years. His slowing down was so gradual that we hardly noticed, but one morning he seemed to have difficulty standing and we had to help him get to his feet.

Once his physical deterioration began, it progressed rapidly. It seemed to pain him to lower his head to drink, so we placed his water container on a box on a level with his head. His eyesight began to fail and he would walk into things. Once he fell into the pool. It was during a period when I was suffering with a bad sciatica nerve and was unable to lift anything, so I lay beside the pool, holding him by the collar until Caroline heard my cries for help and came to our rescue.

Often he was disoriented and could not find his bed at night until one of us would guide him to it. It was at about this time that Jane moved him from his doghouse in the garage to his own room under the house.

"It's safer for him," she reasoned. "And besides, he doesn't have much longer to live."

The room was one we had added on. It is glass on two sides, one looking out onto the pool and the other into a wooded area where my dogwood tree lives. There is a television set in the room, an eight-foot-long sofa, and Jane's collection of classic wicker pieces.

At first Jane tried to discourage Sandy from sleeping on the sofa, but as his arthritis became more and more pronounced, she decided he would be more comfortable there. He was too old now to mount the stairs that led to our living quarters. At first we would sit with him in the downstairs room for a while whenever he seemed lonely. Jane got the idea of leaving the television set on to provide company for him when we were out for the evening. The only indication he ever gave that he was aware of the television was when a dog barked during a drama. Then he would raise his head and utter one guttural warning sound to the intruder and go back to sleep.

We had discussed putting him to sleep and we knew that the time would come. But we were cowards, and we kept giving ourselves excuses not to do it.

"Look how much he enjoys his food," Jane would exclaim. "We can't do it as long as he finds so much pleasure in food."

And so we continued to feed him and, when it became clear that it hurt him to chew his food, Jane would serve him nothing that required him to do more than gum it. Even his dog biscuits had to be soaked in warm water before they were given to him. But he continued to eat and seemed to enjoy his food and so we kept putting off that final trip to Dr. Garner.

And then one morning we went to the downstairs room and Sandy was gone. We always left the door open to the fenced-in side yard so he could relieve himself, but he wasn't out there either. We searched for a hole in the fence where he might have stolen through, but found none. We called him all morning, searched all over our hill, but he was gone, and we never saw him again.

Over the years we have decided that the coyote in Sandy told him that the time had come for him to go, and that he wanted to die on his own terms, in privacy and somewhere out of doors. It is conjecture only. We'll never know for sure.

23. The Miracle of Birth Witnessed!

Once more I longed for the sound of bobwhite quail. Even though we could afford a larger house in a "better" location, we didn't want to leave Avocado Drive. The only thing it lacked as far as I was concerned was the call of the bobwhite quail.

I found an advertisement in a magazine. It was in the back pages where the print is small and where you find ads for compost makers (six tons of recycled garden waste for pennies!) or your life's story put to rhyme for only two dollars. A company in Georgia was offering a "Quail Kit." It included an incubator, twelve fertile bobwhite quail eggs, and a book of instructions. I sent for it.

When the kit arrived, following the directions, I arranged the twelve eggs on the metal grid inside the oval plastic see-through lid, connected it to an electrical outlet and hovered over it. My quail chicks were due to hatch in twenty-one days.

Word that "Earl Hamner is hatching eggs" got around the neighborhood. The younger people on the road were enchanted and would drop by every afternoon after school for a progress report. Some of the older people began looking at me with the same stare Jane's uncle gave me when he found me immersing my hand in the Mississippi River. I didn't care. I had long since become the neighborhood eccentric and it didn't matter what anybody thought of me at this point.

When after thirty days nothing happened, I assumed that nothing would. I cracked one of the eggs, suspecting it was rotten. Inside I found a perfectly formed baby quail, dead and dehydrated. I looked for the egg-beak on its forehead with which it was supposed to have cracked open the egg and released itself. It was there, but had never been put to work. I suspected that I had not provided the proper amount of moisture to the eggs. For that reason the shells remained hard and unyielding, even with the special cutting beak they had developed.

I was discouraged, but determined to try again. This time I bought a professional incubator and set it up on my writing desk directly behind my typewriter where I could keep an eye on it.

For the eggs, I returned to my friend in the west San Fernando Valley who owned the game bird farm. She was still wearing her cap that advertised Alfred Hitchcock's *The Birds* and she recognized me right away.

"You got yourself famous since the last time you were here," she said by way of greeting.

"I didn't realize I was that famous," I said.

"You're that one on *The Waltons*," she said. "The first time I heard it, I recognized your voice. Are all them stories true?"

I explained that some were and some were not, but that most of them had a genesis in some event in my life or the experiences of my family.

"I'm crazy about that Grandpa," she said.

"He's a lovable man," I replied.

"Is he married?"

"I'm afraid so."

"That's a shame," she said. "I could give that man a run for his money."

Once she learned that Will Geer was unavailable, she lost all interest in *The Waltons*.

"How is that rooster I sold you, and the two little hens?" she asked.

I filled her in on the adventures her chickens and I had been having, and she agreed that I had failed in my first attempt by not providing sufficient moisture to the eggs. She sold me twenty-four quail eggs and suggested that if Will Geer's marital status were ever to change, she would appreciate knowing it.

This time I set up my incubator with special care, turning each egg once a day, and keeping a watch on the water level, which I had learned was of the utmost importance. And believing that a watched egg never hatches, I stopped hovering and went back to work.

I was at the *Falcon Crest* production office when Jane

called and said, "You had better get home if you want to see your quail being born." And then she added, "All the other kids in the neighborhood are already here."

Jane's reference to the other kids did not go unnoticed. I had long known that I was considered a peer by every ten-year-old on the street. This came about in part, I think, from the fact that I am a kite fancier. In the days when we had the great open field across from our house, I was there almost every weekend when there was wind, flying one of the kites from my collection.

To this day I have not lived down the fact that a kid named Jeffrey Van Zanten came to the door and asked Jane, "Can Mr. Hamner come out and play?"

At any rate, I arrived home to find that all the other kids in the neighborhood were indeed gathered in my study where they were watching the birth of my quail.

They were in different stages of being hatched. The birth would begin when an egg would give an almost imperceptible quiver. Next the egg would rock ever so slightly. What was causing the movement was the tiny creature inside attempting to saw its way out of the egg shell with its egg tooth.

Once it had sawed a sufficient distance to open the egg, the damp little chick would take a deep breath and expand itself so that the shell would split in two. After an hour or two of hard labor, the tiny thing would lurch about until it had disengaged itself from the shell.

Sympathetic "oh's" and "ah's" would go up from the audience as each quail infant struggled to enter the world.

The effort would exhaust the little bird so that once the egg had split, it would lie there recovering its strength for its next move.

My friend at the bird farm had advised me to prepare some shredded hard-boiled egg yolks for the infants' first meal, so while the newly born chicks were resting up from the trauma of entering the world, I began boiling eggs.

As soon as they could struggle to their feet, they began searching for food and once I placed the egg yolk in the incubator they began to feed.

"Good show, Mr. Hamner," said Jeffrey Van Zanten when the last egg had hatched. I thanked him and then sent all the human youngsters home so that the new arrivals could rest and get acclimated.

Within days their pinfeathers had developed. Within a week they learned to eat a special mash I had bought in addition to the hard-boiled egg yolk. Scott and Caroline helped me with the feeding, but Scott balked at giving them egg yolk. Because they had so recently been egg yolks themselves, he felt it smacked of cannibalism.

From the day they were hatched, I stood by their pen and made the bobwhite call. It seemed to me that they listened. One or two of them would stop in their heedless running around and cock their heads as if something had attracted their attention.

Within about four weeks, they were large enough to be transferred to the elaborate pen I had built for them in the garden house. The pen was about ten feet long and was enclosed with chicken wire. I had built perches and runs, and planted patches of grass and arranged a bird bath for them, and done everything I could to make it a natural habitat. The quail seemed appreciative and at home.

Every night when I arrived home from my office, I began whistling the bobwhite call to them, but there was no answer. And then when they were about three months old I drove up to the garage, parked and began calling to my quail. Did I imagine it or did I hear a faint call reminiscent of bobwhite?

I went to their pen and they came to the wire to greet me, for they had learned to associate me with food. I tried their call, but this time there was no answer. Perhaps they were too interested in the food I had delivered.

Some days later when I drove up in my car and got out, there was a single bird call from the direction of the pen. My heart did a somersault! I had brought Virginia to California. I had re-created a golden moment from my childhood. I had called and my quail had answered me!

Within a week I had only to drive up and stop my car engine to be greeted with a chorus of bobwhites. And by the time I came to their cage, they were waiting to be fed.

They were about four months old when I decided the time had come to release them in the field across from our house. Catching them and transferring them to a cat carrier was no problem because they had lost any fear they might ever have had. When I reached the spot where I planned to release them, I sat beside the cat carrier for a while to allow them to become acclimated. After fifteen minutes or so I opened the door of the container. At first, one little fellow ventured out, and others followed casually. They seemed perfectly at home scratching in the grass for seed and small insects.

When I decided to withdraw, I stood up and quietly began to walk away. The quail continued feeding until one of them spotted me leaving—and came running after me. His action alerted the other birds and they followed until I was being trailed by a procession of twenty-four young quail, all in a straight line, one behind the other in tandem, following me as if I were their mother!

I tried just once to shoo them back into the field, but when they looked to me in confusion I did not have the heart to turn them out into the world. It was just as well, for in minutes every cat in the neighborhood had assembled and were eying my bird-children hungrily. There was even a red-tailed hawk that had spotted them and was circling overhead.

And I knew that after dark the keen noses of the coyotes would smell them out and they would all be gone by the next day.

I brought them all back to their pen where they were safe. For many years they continued to recognize the sound of my car and would welcome me home.

24. The Chicken That Tried to Live Forever!

Not long ago Jane called me at my office. She respects my work and does not interrupt me with business that we can take care of later. I knew that this was no ordinary call.

"Blackie's just about gone," she said. "I'm going to take her to Dr. Garner and get him to put her to sleep."

"I'll meet you there," I said.

"I really can take care of it if you're busy," she said.

"No, I'll be there."

I was working then in my office on Ventura Boulevard, only five minutes from Dr. Garner's office. The project was a new television series for The Family Channel to be filmed in Australia. It was *The Man from Snowy River—The McGregor Saga*, based on the poem by the great Australian poet, Banjo Patterson. I set the script aside and headed for Dr. Garner's office.

Blackie was the last remaining chicken of a clutch of eggs laid by the first bantam hen I had bought. She was to have been the mother of the flock of bobwhite quail I had planned to introduce to the meadow across from our house and thus bring to our California hillside the sounds of my childhood and youth in Virginia.

When Scott and Caroline left home for college, Jane and I became custodians of many of their pets, including Blackie. Blackie remained special. Perhaps it was because her lifetime spanned the childhood of our two children. Perhaps it was simply that Scott and Caroline on their visits home would pay a call to Blackie, would go and sit beside her pen. It was as if they, too, saw the chicken endowed with some mystical connection to their childhood.

Because of her longevity, many of our friends knew of Blackie's existence and when we would see those friends and neighbors we would encounter only rarely, such as at Christmas or New Year's, they never failed to marvel that Blackie was still alive.

Blackie had lived an astonishing number of years. We figured she was in her eighteenth or nineteenth year before she began to show signs of age and disability. She began to lose feathers and develop bald spots. Eventually the entire back of her head became bald, which gave her a vulture-like appearance.

As her strength waned, we noticed that she remained on the ground at night instead of flying up to the roost we had arranged in her pen. In earlier years, she made a rather jaunty figure there, because we had placed an old purple umbrella over the roost to protect her from the elements. Often she would peer out from under the umbrella and the look in her beady little eyes would seem to say: "Have you no respect for a lady's privacy?" But now she was too old. She would attempt to fly up to the roost, but she simply didn't have the strength to make it. It soon became part of my routine each night on arriving home from work to go down to Blackie's pen and lift her up on her roost. She seemed grateful; certainly she was more comfortable sleeping under her purple umbrella where she had slept for the last eighteen or so years.

At night we would help her up, but then it became apparent that she did not have the strength to fly back down to the ground in the morning. She would sit there all day unless Jane or I went down and lifted her down.

Once on the ground, she would wander vacantly around, pecking at food that wasn't there or failing to grasp in her beak the food that was. She became increasingly feeble and disoriented. We knew that the end was not far away, but we decided, as we had with Sandy, that as long as she found any pleasure in life that we would not put her to sleep. Her one pleasure seemed to be food, so we would feed her by hand. We would hold out grain until, piece by piece, she managed to eat enough to sustain life for another day.

More and more frequently when we would go to check on her, we would find that Blackie had fallen. She would be on the ground, a desperate look in her eye, the stricken look of a creature that knows it does not have long to live, but still is reluctant to let go of life.

We kept looking for ways to avoid the inevitable. Aside

from our own sentimental reasons, Blackie's life force had been so strong. She had endured for so many years. She had known life for such an unusually long time. But we were cowards. Secretly we wished that she might pass on quietly in her sleep.

At the breakfast table we would say, "Wonder how that old chicken is this morning?" All the while we knew what our secret wish had been. We would go to her pen hopefully, but there the pathetic old thing would be, still clinging to her roosting pole and to life. We would place her back down on the ground to spend another day pecking at grain that wasn't there.

Then the day arrived when Jane called me at my office. Jane's whole life is based on affirmation, and I knew that if a woman who had taught squirrels to urinate, revived infant hamsters from death, and brought solace to arthritic and dying dogs, felt that the time had come, then I had no choice but to join her in helping Blackie take leave of her burdensome life.

Jane had arrived ahead of me at Dr. Garner's office. She was already in the waiting room and was holding Blackie, who was wrapped in a towel and who no longer had the strength to even hold her head erect.

Dr. Garner is a kind and considerate man. He sensed the distress Jane and I were going through.

"Blackie looks like she's just about had it," he observed.

"We think it's time to put her to sleep," said Jane.

Dr. Garner looked to me, and I nodded in agreement.

He took Blackie from Jane and disappeared into the back of the hospital.

Jane and I sat quietly together until he came back into the waiting room.

"She's gone," he said.

Numbly we made our way down the corridor to the alley at the back of the building. It was only when we were in the parking lot that we turned to each other, embraced and both burst into tears.

And we wept, not that a chicken was dead, but that a door had closed and our last slender link with our children as children, was gone.

Of course, it is tremendously gratifying that there is a handsome and talented young man named Scott who is a fine writer. He comes to see us and is tolerant and amused by two slightly daffy older folks who are his parents. It is equally gratifying that there is a meltingly beautiful, loving, and gifted young family therapist named Caroline, who visits and explains the lyrics of popular songs to us and is touchingly concerned about my fading memory and her mother's health.

Scott and Carrie have their own homes now, and their own lives, but sometimes at sundown, I look across the garden and I see a little girl carrying in a Mason jar a snail named Susie Green. Beside her walks a little boy who carries a recently hatched baby chick. He has just named her Blackie.

About the Author

Earl Hamner is best known as the creator and producer of *The Waltons*, the long-running television series based on his memories of growing up in the foothills of Virginia's Blue Ridge Mountains. The creator and producer of *Falcon Crest* and other television series, he also wrote many episodes of *The Twilight Zone*. As a film writer, he won awards for *Where the Lilies Bloom* and for the adaptation of the E.B. White classic *Charlotte's Web*.

He and his wife, Jane, live in Studio City, California.

Printed in the USA
CPSIA information can be obtained
at www.ICGtesting.com
JSHW082200140824
68134JS00014B/339

9 781620 454947